THE WINEMAKER'S COMPANION

THE WINEMAKER'S COMPANION

A handbook for those who make wine at home

BY

B. C. A. TURNER

President, National Association of
Amateur Winemakers

C. J. J. BERRY

Editor of
The Amateur Winemaker

A. I. MARSHALL

North American Editor

MILLS & BOON TORONTO - LONDON
101 DUNCAN MILL ROAD,
DON MILLS, CANADA.

First published 1960
Second edition 1963
Reprinted 1965 and 1967 (revised)
Reprinted 1968, 1970
Reprinted 1971 (revised)
© *B. C. A. Turner and C. J. J. Berry 1960*

ISBN 263-51732-2

International edition first published 1972
by Mills & Boon, Toronto-London
101 Duncan Mill Rd., Don Mills, Canada

ACKNOWLEDGMENTS

The Authors wish to acknowledge the debt of gratitude they
owe to:

1. Messrs. J. O'Brien and A. K. Whitley, for the assistance
they gave in connection with the chapter on Beer. Facilities
were most kindly provided for study in a famous brewery and
the chapter was subsequently checked for accuracy.

2. S. C. Goddard, Esq., B.Sc., who very generously checked
the whole manuscript for scientific accuracy.

Printed and bound in Canada.

CONTENTS

Chapter		Page

LIST OF ILLUSTRATIONS

PREFACE

A NUMBER of books have now been published on the subject of making wine at home, and we owe a great deal to the pioneers who stimulated interest after the war, usually with Great-grandma's recipes. During recent years, however, there has been a trend towards a more scientific approach. Specialized equipment has become available to the amateur (notably the fermentation lock, wine yeasts and yeast nutrients), and consequently there have been great strides in winemaking knowledge. An experienced winemaker can now produce exactly the kind and type of wine he or she wants, with an assuredness far from the hit-or-miss methods known till now.

A large number of recipes, including some less well known, are given at the back, but this book is unlike others in that the recipes are not of major importance. The prime purpose in producing this book is to make available to every winemaker full and up-to-date information on every aspect of the making of wine, in a form suitable for quick reference; admittedly with some technicalities, but in a language that can be readily understood by the non-scientist.

While the chapters follow a logical sequence in theory and practice they have been written, as far as possible, complete in themselves so that reference to any particular chapter does not necessitate too many cross references. As a result certain essential facts have been repeated, but they are so important, we feel that no apology need be offered.

This is not a scientific treatise for the specialist, nor does it go to the other extreme. It is intended for the hundreds of thousands of practical winemakers in town and country, abroad as well as at home, who are keen to improve the quality of their wine as much as possible within their circumstances.

Those who use this book will find that they can make superb wine that costs but a "song".

Chapter 1

BACKGROUND TO WINEMAKING

I T IS most interesting to record that at a time when the standard of living is rising, and when, with regrettable exceptions, most families have never been so well off, there is an enormous increase in the custom of making wine at home. This pursuit is by no means confined to those who like to drink wine often but find the commercial wine sold at the local stores too expensive for frequent purchase. Nor is it confined to the inhabitants of country cottages who might be thought to have a less sophisticated palate. Fortunately for all of us, some of these good souls continued making wine year by year, generation by generation, and kept alive knowledge of the basic principles of our art.

The majority of winemakers, in Great Britain at least, are men and women of intelligence and culture, often members of the so-called middle classes. They could certainly afford to purchase some wine ready made, but they have found that they can make, often for as little as 15¢ a bottle, wine at least as good as they can buy and often better. Great satisfaction and pleasure are obtained during the creative process of making wine. Furthermore the discipline of patience while waiting for the wine to mature leads the amateur vintner to approach the consummation with a reverence appropriate to wine . . . first to inspect, then to smell, and finally to taste with a serious, critical consideration by no means alien to enjoyment and conviviality and certainly conducive to appreciation.

Our word wine comes, not from the French "vin" as so many people think, but from the Greek word "oinos", for the Greeks were making wine 3,000 years ago when the French, like ourselves, were still barbarians. And let there be no mistake, the Greeks did not mean by "oinos" wine made only from the fermented juice of the grape. On the contrary, the word "oinos" was a generic title which often included wine made from other ingredients. The Greeks have never been purists in this matter and still make and sell wine from ingredients other than pure grape juice. There is, however, another Greek word "oine" which means vine and there is an obvious connection between "oine" and "oinos". In the main the Greeks clearly made most of their wine from grapes. But there is no doubt that "wine" is nowadays, as it was 3,000 years ago, a generic term covering a wide variety of fermented drinks. The *Oxford Dictionary*, while saying that wine is "fermented grape juice", also concedes that "wine" is the appropriate description for a "fermented drink,

11

resembling wine, made from specified fruit, etc. (cowslip, goose-berry, orange, palm wine and so on)".

The claim that only fermented grape juice is wine has been fostered and built up in recent centuries. It has certainly been strengthened by legislation in the wine-producing countries. This legislation has been necessary to protect great national indus-tries from malpractice by unscrupulous vignerons. For example it was common custom, until the mid nineteenth century, to add elderberries to port wine to improve the colour and streng-then the flavour—which of course says much for elderberries, and, by the same token, for elderberry wine. In England, too, irregular additions were sometimes made by dishonest mer-chants. The leaders of national wine industries have quite pro-perly set high and rigid standards for their members to follow, with which even the most enthusiastic amateur winemake cannot but agree.

In all the great wine-producing countries legislation has been passed defining wine as the product from the fermentation of the juice of fresh grapes. It is universally agreed that grapes can often (though not always) be made into good wine and that the great European vignerons, with centuries of continuous ex-perience and rich blessings of sun, soil and situation, can some-times make a wine that may be remembered for a lifetime. But the time has now come to establish another fact. With the better understanding provided by modern scientific knowledge of ex-actly what happens in the process of making wine, an excellent "fermented drink" can be made at home that will have a per-sonality and individuality of its own, able to compare most fa-vourably with standard commercial wines. It should be remem-bered by those who speak ill of our country wines, that they are comparing our wine not with the "vin du pays" or "vin ordinaire", made by the individual peasant and which they may have drunk almost without noticing what they were drinking; but with the wines that they can remember. Naturally the wines that can be remembered are among the finest produced. Wines made at home can occasionally match these fine wines in de-licacy of bouquet and flavour, but in the main, like the people of other lands, we make our wine for everyday use. The amateur winemaker, unlike his commercial colleagues, has no prejudices about his wine. He enjoys all good wine, whether it has been made from "the juice of fresh grapes" or the soft fruit of his own garden. And because of the ancient and now modern ge-neric meaning of the word, he can legitimately call it wine.

Archaelogists have established that wine was first made at least 10,000 years ago, and mead makers will rejoice to learn that it is thought to be almost certain that honey was fermented centuries earlier. By the time of the incredible Egyptian civilization, wine was widely made and drunk. Strip pictures in the ancient tombs show us details of every aspect of the art. Incidentally, art it was, for only in the last century has science been introduced. It is comforting to think that the slaves who built the pyramids were perhaps supported by their ration of date wine; the Nile Valley is not now suitable for grape vines, although it seems likely that many thousands of years ago there were in fact some vineyards there. At that time it is probable that the making of wine was the prerogative of the Pharaoh, for few others had access to the ingredients or the opportunity. He, no doubt, employed a winemaker-in-chief with a staff of assistants, and a substantial quantity was made, some of which may have been sold or bartered. In later centuries it is quite certain that there was much individuality in making wine. By the time of the Marriage Feast of Cana and especially the Last Supper there can be no doubt that the wine, like the bread, was made by some member of the family. It may not have been very good wine by modern standards of perfection, but it was certainly wine.

The Christian Church has accordingly always had a great interest in wine and the great religious orders have contributed much to the sum total of our wine knowledge and to present standards. Every monastery had its cellarer whose duty, among others, was to provide good sound wine not only for sacramental purposes but also for the refreshment of the monks and their guests. Certain innovators experimented with distillation and with the addition of herbs and flavours at some stage or another. Gradually special drinks, now called liqueurs, were evolved that have become famous, such as "Benedictine", first made by the monks of the order of St. Benedict, and "Chartreuse", originally made by the Carthusian monks. Many other religious names are connected with winemaking on the Continent, such as the Hospice de Beaune, a charity founded for the sick poor as long ago as 1441, Château-neuf-du-Pape, which goes back to the days when the true Pope resided at Avignon, while the false was in Rome, and Liebfraumilch, the name given to a wine originally made in the vineyards adjacent to the Church of Our Lady, in a suburb of Worms on the Rhine, to mention only three. What is important to remember is that in the beginning all these now famous wines were made only in small quantities, for use in the monastery, the château or the schloss, and the wine eventually became world famous because of the high quality achieved by the individual vintner. Only in recent centuries has wine growing on such an enormous commercial scale developed.

With the great social changes attendant on the industrial revolution this custom of making wine for the family declined and almost died out. Tea was introduced and found to be a more soothing beverage for the harassed worker than wine, which needs a mind free from worry and care to be fully enjoyed. Gin was produced so cheaply that one could get drunk for a penny! There was little opportunity for the vast majority of people either to drink wine or to make their own wine. Those who could afford to do so drank imported wines.

At the turn of this century, however, things began to improve, and just before the Second World War a few enthusiasts began to make their own wines from recipes handed down by folk who lived in the country, where money was still scarce but where fruit and flowers were abundant. European wines were so cheap, however, that it was really hardly worth the time and trouble. And then the war came. Wine imports virtually ceased and the price of wine became prohibitive. For years sugar was rationed and the enthusiasts were able to make only very small quantities of wine, which they naturally kept in the family.

With the introduction of the Welfare State, another social revolution began. There was more time for leisure, and after such a long period of carnage, destruction and privation, there was a very widespread desire to do something creative for a change. Because of the high cost of living many people began to do for themselves jobs about the house that ten years previously they would not have considered. A new phrase was coined—"Do it yourself". It applied not only to house repairs and decoration but to innumerable other activities, including, of course, making wine. The taste for wine had been developed by hundreds of thousands during service abroad, in places where wines were cheap and plentiful. The circumstances had arisen for a return to the old family custom of making one's own wine. At first no doubt the wines were not too well made and certainly were drunk too soon. But as soon as more information became available the standards began to rise. The inquiring mind is now able to find the answer from modern scientific knowledge to the problems of making quality wine.

In 1954 the first association of winemakers was inaugurated in Andover and the idea has rapidly spread throughout England. Tastings and competitions afford yardsticks by which to judge our efforts and something new is constantly being learned. The most important developments have been in the use of yeast nutrient, acids and tannin, in selected yeast strains for fermentation, in the use of the hydrometer to determine the correct quantity of sugar required for the kind of wine being made, and, perhaps the most important, in the use of the fermentation lock to save our musts from becoming vinegar instead of wine. These items will be discussed in detail later on, but in the meantime a mental note should be made to give them special attention. They can hardly be over-emphasized, for they control the very quality of our wine.

There are as yet no national standards for our guidance. Some winemakers try to imitate foreign commercial wines in name as well as in nature and describe their wines as "blackberry port" or "gooseberry champagne". Others go to the opposite extreme of modernity and, perhaps reminiscent of their army days, describe their wines as "jungle juice" or "tiger's milk". The latter titles, we feel, are to be deprecated lest they bring our craft into bad odour and ill repute, and lead to its being regarded as something childish, undignified and unworthy of serious consideration. We feel too that we have no need, necessarily, to copy commercial names and that our wines are in fact able to stand up for comparison under their own local names, whether they be apple wine or something else. On the other hand too much importance should not be attached to nomenclature. Our wines are made for our own enjoyment and not for sale, so it really matters little what we call them.

We in Great Britain are nowadays so closely associated with North Americans that it is worth recording that in spite of the publicity of the soft drinks industry, an enormous amount of grape and fruit wine is regularly made both commercially and privately in the States and Canada. Grapes are grown almost everywhere, although the industry is concentrated mainly in California and Ontario. Many research chemists study the problems of vinification exclusively and a leading authority, Professor W. E. V. Cruess, includes a special chapter on fruit wines in the second edition of his book, *The Principles and Practice of Winemaking*. This is only an indication of the widespread interest in America of making wine at home.

National standards are well established in Germany, Poland, Yugoslavia and other countries where fruit and flower wines are made regularly not only by thousands of individual families, but by commercial firms as well. There is no reason why we cannot achieve the same high standards and make for our own enjoyment a variety of wines of similar quality. Even English legislation is co-operative, for there is no restriction at all upon the making of wine at home, *provided it is consumed privately and not offered for sale.*

It is however, quite properly, an offence against the law to distil, i.e. to make alcohol at home. Unless you are a qualified chemist with adequate laboratory facilities it can be extremely dangerous to health to drink the distillation of wine. Yeast ferments sugar into at least four different alcohols, all of which may be present in wine in different quantities and for different useful and beneficial purposes. Further details will be given later. At present suffice it to say that some of these alcohols, though beneficial in minute quantities, are most injurious in the larger doses which are obtained by distillation. It must be emphasized then that it is both illegal and dangerous to distil at home. Furthermore, it would be positively wasteful, for most wine is good, even if some is better than others, and a great quantity of good wine has to be used to obtain a small quantity of inferior alcohol. Far rather, then, drink some of this wine every day and add lustre to your health and luxury to your victuals.

Chapter 2

EQUIPMENT

T HE IMPRESSIVE list of equipment which follows is unlikely to be possessed by anyone in its entirety. Nor, indeed, is it all *essential* to the making of good sound wine. Nevertheless, there are many winemakers who take their hobby just as seriously as certain photographers, anglers, artists and so on. Such winemakers are not concerned with the production of a palatable wine to serve with their Sunday lunch, but with the creation of a work of art. For them the pleasure is in the making perhaps more than in the drinking, just as the angler, with his waders, his fly-stuck hat, his several rods and so on, enjoys the actual fishing in expensive, privately owned water, more than the fish he catches, which he may not even eat.

Every item mentioned has a particular usefulness, but except for those which are obviously essential, they can be added one or two at a time as your inclination suggests. Certain items are already in every house, others can be made by the handyman and the remainder can now be bought from a variety of firms in different parts of the country.

For the sake of convenience and to avoid unnecessary repetition the list is compiled in order of use as far as this is possible.

MASHING VESSELS

Buckets, open-necked jars or containers made from polyethylene are ideally suitable for mashing. The material is completely resistant to acids and alkalis, is easy to clean, unbreakable and very light in weight. This is important when 2 or 3 gals. of wine or even more are being prepared. An Imperial gallon of water weighs 10 lbs. and to this you must add the weight of fruit, possibly also the sugar and the container. A 4-gal. brew in an earthenware crock or wooden half-cask can weigh well over 50 lb., and it is when you are handling heavy and awkward containers that accidents are most likely to occur. Furthermore a polyethylene bucket, with graduations on the inside up to 1½ gals., costs under $1. Polyethylene garbage pails, up to 20 Imperial gals. (90 litres), are well worth using. They can be thoroughly recommended.

Other types of mashing vessels are often used. A wooden tub with a lid, sometimes known as an open halfcask, can be obtained for mashing in sizes to hold from 2 to 5 gals. It is important that it should not have previously contained any substance likely to be injurious to wine. At all times it should be kept thoroughly clean, since the grain of the wood and the joints of the staves form a natural home for moulds and bacteria. The main advantage of wooden tubs is that they are very strong and unlikely to break if dropped or knocked over. A wooden masher can be used with them safely. On the other hand they are very heavy and rather expensive.

Stone or earthenware glazed crocks, bung jars or "grey hens", are also very heavy, but they have the advantage that the internal glaze is very easy to keep clean. Care must be taken in their use since they might break, crack or chip if dropped or knocked over. They cost only about a quarter as much as the wooden tubs and can be obtained in sizes from 1 gal. upwards. New crocks are certain to be safely glazed, but if an Oriental or a very old crock is obtained, the glaze should be inspected to ensure that the clay has not been covered with a lead glaze, which of course would react with the acids in the must and poison the brew. A lead glaze looks thick, opaque and honey-coloured, a salt or modern glaze is thin and transparent.

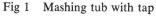

Fig 1   Mashing tub with tap   Fig 2   Mashing jar

A preserving pan or fish-kettle is needed for those ingredients which have to be boiled. An iron vessel may be used provided it is heavily enamelled and the enamel is in perfect condition, but once again the weight is against it. An aluminium pan is light and perfectly suitable and so too are the tin fish-kettles, provided they are sound and not rusty, and that liquids are not left in them for several hours.

When fruit has to be broken up, a wooden masher can be very helpful. It should be made from clean well-seasoned ash or oak, and may be square or round. In essentials it is a balk of wood, perhaps 1 ft. long and 2 to 3 ins. wide with a handle in one end—a piece of broomstick also 1 ft. long does admirably. At a pinch a rolling pin would serve quite well instead.

When making up equipment of any sort involving wood or metal, care should be taken in the selection of the material. Resinous woods such as pine, or any other wood which has a natural smell or a colour that is likely to be bleached, should be avoided. Apart from stainless steel, aluminium or tin, no metal should be allowed to come into contact with liquids containing acids and the aluminium should be virtually pure with only a very small percentage of alloy for strengh. The tin should have a thorough coating and be in a polished condition.

These remarks apply also to wooden spoons, mincers, colanders, knives and chopping boards. If two pieces of wood have to be joined together it is better to use wooden dowels, rather than nails, screws or glue.

STRAINING

After mashing the must is strained and for this purpose it is most important to use a strong cloth with a very fine weave. Butter muslin can be used but it is not really suitable because the weave is too open and several thicknesses will be required to hold back the pulp. A good quality linen will do provided it is 3 or 4 ft. square. Nylon sieves are excellent but need to be of as large a size as possible. The weave is very fine, the material is very strong, washes cleanly and easily and dries quickly. Jelly bags can also be used and it is sometimes an advantage to use a colander for a preliminary straining.

When the cloth has to be squeezed to extract the juice it is a good idea to wear a pair of household rubber gloves. After you have put them on rinse your gloved hands in hot water to make sure they are thoroughly clean before handling the cloth. These gloves prove extremely useful when making, for example, elderberry wine. Elderberry juice stains your hands a dark colour, especially under the finger-nails.

It is always useful to have a variety of funnels in different sizes, and a very large one is particularly useful. Glass funnels are quite suitable but extremely liable to breakage, and although aluminium or enamelled funnels may also be used with confidence, the polyethylene funnels seem to have all the advantages. They are quite inexpensive, too. Funnels can also be fitted with loose strainers.

FERMENTATION VESSELS

Fermentation vessels provide us with a wide choice and can now be obtained with either narrow or wide necks, with airtight closures. For easy cleaning the latter are more desirable. Oak wine-casks are excellent though expensive. The optimum size for use at home is 5 gals. They are somewhat awkward to sterilize compared with other vessels and need a separate stand since there would be seepage if the staves were in contact with a solid surface. They possess advantages of durability and of ease in use when you have the knack of them, and admit a small amount of beneficial air to the wine through the pores of the wood. A drilled wooden bung is required for the bung-hole and a spile peg for the drill hole. During fermentation an air-lock is used in the drill hole and this is replaced by the spile after fermentation. It must, of course, be replaced with a porous spile when the wooden tap is inserted in the tap hole prior to drawing the finished wine off the less for bottling.

Stoneware jars or barrels, with or without tap holes and taps, are excellent. They are easily cleaned and sterilized and can be stood in any warm corner. They are less than half the cost of wine-casks. For the smaller house with fewer facilities the most effective container for fermenting must is undoubtedly the glass jar seen on Plate I. Two sizes are available: ½ gal. and 1 gal., and the latter is the one to use. A ½ gal. is really too small a quantity to produce good results from the fermentation. They are easy to handle and to clean, but subject to the normal fragility of glass. On the other hand, you can see what is going on in the jar and they are cheap. Fermented wine has to be siphoned off the lees, but siphoning is quite simple.

The larger the quantity of wine fermented in one container the better the wine, and sometimes glass carboys holding 4½ to 5 Imperial gals. can be obtained.

Polyethylene jars can also be bought with narrow necks and are, of course, excellent in every way: they are relatively expensive but have a much longer life. Over the years it is worth while getting together a variety, in different sizes, of all these containers mentioned, for they each have their special advantages of which you can make use as you see fit for any particular wine.

A mallet should be kept with the wooden taps and bungs so that it is readily available when wanted. It is unwise to hit a wooden tap with a metal hammer since there is a danger that this might split the tap.

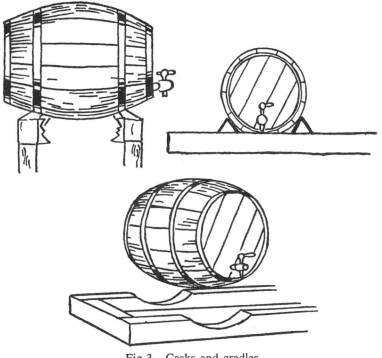

Fig 3   Casks and cradles

Fig 4   Storage jar with tap

FERMENTATION LOCKS

Fermentation traps are known as the "winemakers' best friend" and detailed information will be given about their use in a subsequent chapter. The most used type of trap consists of a piece of glass tube about ¼ in. in diameter bent to form a loop and with bubbles blown in each upright of the U as in Fig. 5. They are quite fragile and need great care in handling, especially since they are somewhat expensive. There are also plastic types which work quite well, and are comparatively cheap and more durable. It is not so easy to see the bubbles of carbon dioxide passing through these locks, however, and many winemakers *do* like to be able to follow the progress of fermentation. An improved version is the Emil fermentation lock which is made in two parts. The first consists only of a bent glass tube passed through a bored cork. There is much less likelihood of breaking this when pressing the cork into the neck of the jar, the time when most locks are broken.

The second piece consists of another section of glass tube passed through a smaller grooved cork fitted into a test-tube containing water. A short piece of rubber tubing joins the first glass tube to the second. The groove down the side of the small cork enables the gas which bubbles through the water to escape.

Fig 5   Fermentation lock fitted in 1-gallon jar

Simple versions of this lock can be made at home for next to nothing, using empty yeast tablet phials, tiny aspirin bottles or the like.

CORKS AND CORKING

The large cork which fits into the fermentation jar needs to be very close fitting and neatly bored so that the glass tube also fits snugly. It is important to achieve a completely airtight fit throughout, and for the fermentation bottles themselves rubber stoppers are slightly superior, because they are not porous at all and the hole is drilled during manufacture. They are more easily sterilized too, but cost three times as much as the cork. If corks are used in preference to rubber stoppers they should be covered in paraffin wax or candle grease to make them airtight. The wax should be pressed into the tiny gap where the glass tube enters the cork and also where the cork enters the jar. Unbored corks should also be available in quantity and in different sizes for your various jars and bottles. Larger ones will be required for the jars.

Bottle corks can be obtained either with a cap for easy removal, when they are known as stoppers, or cylindrical for driving home flush. The latter type give a neat finish to the bottle, especially when a plastic or foil capsule is used. Plastic stoppers are now available and are cheap and excellent to use. They can be sterilized without difficulty, contract easily when inserting and expand to a good fit. They have a cap for easy removal and may be used repeatedly. Their only slightly higher cost is mitigated by their efficiency and long life.

Plastic capsules can be used only once and must be kept soft in a little of the liquid in which they are supplied. They quickly dry hard and have to be torn off when the bottle is opened. The tinfoil capsules are perhaps a little more attractive and can occasionally be used a second time, but they do not form a seal like the plastic capsule, which adheres to the neck of the bottle. Both types of capsule can be obtained in several colours; the foil in red, gold and silver, the plastic in all the hues of the rainbow.

If you intend to bore your own corks it is advisable to use the special cork borer available for this purpose. An ordinary twist drill breaks away the side of the hole and leaves an untidy jagged gap. The cork borer consists of a hollow metal tube about ¼ in. in diameter, sharpened at one end and crossed with a T-bar at the other. The cork to be bored should be inserted not too tightly in an empty bottle or jar to hold it firmly while the borer is being turned as you would a gimlet. If the cork is pressed into the jar too lightly it will be compressed so much that upon removal the hole may be found to be too large.

There are a number of gadgets to assist you in getting a cork right home. The simplest and least expensive is a piece of plastic-covered wire no more than 1/16 in. in diameter and about 8 or 10 ins. long. The wire is inserted with the cork, which can be pressed with the heel of your hand, and when right home the wire is withdrawn, bringing with it a small quantity of compressed air, which would otherwise force the cork up a little. The next most common aid is a simple cork flogger, consisting of a length of hard wood about 4 ins. wide and narrowing down to the handle. A mallet may also be used, of course.

Fig 6　"Flogger"

A neat machine costing about $2 consists of a wooden cylinder with a plunger passing through it. There is a hole in the

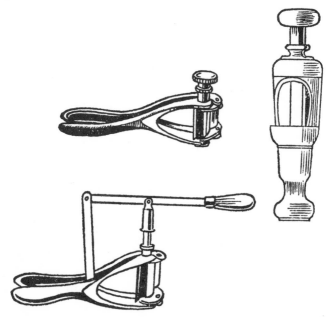

Fig 7　Corking devices

side of the cylinder in which the cork is inserted. The cylinder is shaped to compress the cork as it passes through when pushed by the plunger, the top of which is hit by a flogger or mallet.

There are at least three Sanbri corking machines, working on the same principles but replacing the blow on the plunger by pressure on a lever. A bench model quickly and simply corks a considerable number of bottles with the minimum of effort. The hand models are equally effective if somewhat slower. A corking machine is a real help if you are bottling more than 2 or 3 gals. of wine at a time. You have to make a substantial blow with a flogger or mallet and there is always the possibility for the inexperienced of mis-hitting, and perhaps bruising the hand, or worse, breaking the bottle!

While discussing corks, mention may be made of wire loops, which can now be bought to hold corks down against a pressure of gas in sparkling or champagne-type wines. The loop of wire is passed over the neck of the bottle; the two ends are brought up over the cork and separated to give two separate holdings, then down the other side, under the wire, pulled hard, twisted together and pressd up flat to the bottle.

As mentioned, barrels need bungs and these are made of oak slightly chamfered so that they can be driven home flush to form an integral part of the stave. They are removed by banging on the neighbouring staves. This loosens the bung and it can be lifted out. A screwdriver or similar metal instrument should *not* be used to prise up the bung as this will damage the bung and the hole, so that the airtight fit is lost. The spile used in conjunction with the bung is about 2 ins. long and ¼ in. in diameter. It is sharpened at one end.

LABELS

Labels are an essential in some form or another. For home use with bottles that will not be taken to table (because the wine is served in a decanter), a simple sticky label 1¼ by ¾ in. is sufficient with just the name and the date. For bottles that you may give to friends and exhibit in public a printed label some 3 by 2 ins. should be used. They can be obtained already printed with the name of the wine or with the space blank for you to inscribe the details. Many wine clubs print their own labels cheaply and if you are a member you can no doubt have some say in how they shall look. There are also on the market decorative china labels bearing the name of the wine suspended on a chain which you simply hang over the neck of your decanter or bottle. Corks with decorative china heads and the name of the wine are also available for the bottle you are using at the moment.

There has been some divergence to take in all the corks, bungs, labels, etc., arising from the drilled corks for the fermentation traps. But before fermentation starts you will want to be sure that your must has all the necessary ingredients to become the wine you wish to make.

HYDROMETERS AND OTHER INSTRUMENTS

The first and most important test is with the hydrometer, to ascertain the specific gravity of your must. The detail of the purpose and practical use of the hydrometer will be dealt with fully in Chapter 9.

If you intend to be accurate in your hydrometer readings, you should also use a thermometer, for the scale on the hydrometer will be graduated at a certain prescribed temperature indicated at the top of the scale. At temperatures above or below that prescribed, additions or subtractions must be made as indicated later. The thermometer may be an ordinary water thermometer with a scale from freezing to boiling or a special wine thermometer, graduated only from freezing to 100° F (38° C). If the latter is used, it should never be placed in hot water, or it will burst. The thermometer has, of course, many other uses in winemaking and is a really worthwhile piece of equipment to have.

Another "ometer" that is useful to the winemaker is the vinometer. This consists of a slender glass capillary tube about 4½ ins. long under a small thistle-shaped funnel. The tube is graduated 0-25. The vinometer is used for ascertaining the quantity of alcohol in a wine. The capillary tube is filled with wine through the funnel—only a few drops are needed—and is then upturned on to a flat surface. The wine runs down the tube and stops at a point on the scale equal to the percentage of alcohol in the wine by volume. The instrument works simply by the variation of the surface tension of the meniscus and with a dry wine is reasonably accurate. Unfortunately with sweet wines there seems usually to be a tendency towards very high alcohol readings, if one checks results with those obtained with the hydrometer or by laboratory distillation, so the vinometer is really only of use with dry wines. Calculating the alcohol content by hydrometer readings, taken before and after fermentation, is certainly the most accurate, simple method open to most of us, who have no access to a laboratory and are hardly likely to be able to afford an Ebullioscope, the instrument used commercially.

The hydrometer, trial jar, thermometer and vinometer are all delicate scientific instruments that need to be used very care-

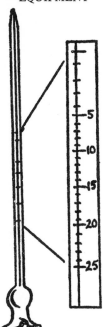

Fig 8   Vinometer

fully and kept spotlessly clean and sterile and stored in some safe place (away from the reach of children), where they are unlikely to be broken by accident.

CHEMICALS

Certain chemicals are very useful to have handy, notably of course Campden tablets. This is the proprietary preparation of potassium metabisulphite used in sterilization. These tablets are very convenient to use, for each one contains exactly 7 grains. Just 1 tablet in a gallon or 5 litres of liquid is usually sufficient.

Yeast nutrients should always be available either in the ready prepared tablet form, which can be bought in phials of 8 for 25¢. In the natural state the combination of chemicals is hygroscopic, i.e. absorbs moisture from the air, and becomes messy to handle. Known quantities should be kept in solution so that it is possible to use precise portions to the gallon of must. A small jar of yeast energizer and an ounce of pectic enzyme are well worth keeping.

A small phial of dried grape tannin is useful on occasions and also some citric acid. Fresh lemon juice can be used instead, but it is not always possible to have fresh lemons on hand just when they are needed. The juice of 8 average lemons equals one ounce (30 grams) of citric acid.

FILTERS AND SIPHONS

A packet of unmedicated cotton wool is worth keeping in your winery. Test-tubes containing growing yeast cultures have to be plugged with cotton wool, as do jars in which sherry-type wine is fermented. The cotton wool acts as a filter for the air entering the jar or tube; it can also be used as an emergency wine filter. In storage it should be kept sterile and well protected from contamination.

Sometimes a wine has to be filtered after fermentation. Asbestos pulp is the best medium, effective and easy to use.

Filterpapers are not very successful because they are so slow, and both pulp and paper are improved if used in conjunction with a filter pump. This can be bought as a small unit to attach to the kitchen tap. (See illustration.) When the tap is turned on the running water draws out the air from the conical flask and creates a partial vacuum in it. As nature abhors a vacuum the wine is sucked through the filter-paper or asbestos pulp into the flask at a faster rate than gravity alone could provide.

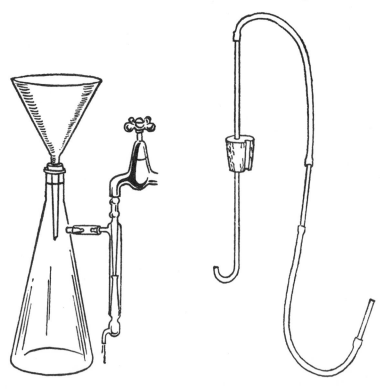

Fig 9   Filter pump   Fig 10   Siphon

To avoid filtering you can use a fining agent. Isinglass is often recommended, as are milk, blood, albumen, beaten white of egg or gelatine, but isinglass is very tricky and unreliable.

As soon as the precipitate has settled the clear wine should be racked and this is best done by siphoning. The siphon need consist of nothing but a 4-ft. length of rubber tubing, but this can be much improved by the inclusion of two pieces of glass tubing (one of them a U-tube) and a spring clip Alternatively a commercial siphon may be purchased which includes a suction pump attachment.

BRUSHES

Bottle brushes are very useful to have in variety. A long-handled one to reach down to the bottom of jars and bottles and one with a bent head to get at the shoulders of jars, where very often there is a line of yeast sediment. Some silver sand will occasionally be found useful to clean obstinate marks in jars and bottles. Mechanical brushes with steel or bronze brush heads can be bought to do the really dirty work very efficiently, and for the winemaker with a large number of dirty bottles to clean there is a rotary bottle washing machine.

STORAGE

Storage of bottles is the next problem, and wineracks can be bought in metal or wood ready made for the purpose. Odd corners can be built up specially either by yourself or a local carpenter. The supports may be made from lengths of 1-in. square wood about 14 in. long balanced on one edge and screwed to uprights in such a fashion that each bottle is supported by two sides of the squared wood, see Fig. 16. Barrels must be supported on something like the framework of a stool.

Chapter 3

THE BASIC PRINCIPLES

W HATEVER THE stage of your experience in winemaking it is a great help to have clear in your mind the broad, general outline of the craft, to have some idea of what you are trying to accomplish, before studying in detail the means to achieve these ends. The purpose of this chapter is to give you that broad picture, to explain the general principles of winemaking, or vinification, to use a more technical term. Anyone can make wine, of a sort, by following a simple recipe. It may turn out well, but it is by no means certain and you are more likely to produce a quality wine if you have studied the principles involved and applied them carefully.

The central and most important single aspect of winemaking is, of course, the fermentation. It is during this process that alcohol is formed, the essential ingredient of wine. What causes fermentation? A clue is to be found in the word itself, for in Latin "fermentum" is "that which causes fermentation, leaven, *yeast*".

Fermentation can best be explained by saying simply that when yeast, which is a living organism is put into a sugary solution it feeds upon the sugar, and in doing so converts it approximately half to alcohol and half to carbon dioxide. In a suitable solution, the yeast will continue to ferment the sugar until so much alcohol has been produced that the concentration is sufficient to inhibit it from further action—this is usually somewhere between 14%–18% alcohol by volume. Yeast cells die after reproducing themselves some thirty times or so, but even after its death the yeast has still a contribution to make, for by a complex autolysis beyond the scope of this work, part of it is then converted into a nutrient for that yeast which is still alive.

Some varieties of yeast, it should be noted, can stand a higher concentration of alcohol than others; they are said to have a greater alcoholic tolerance and it is naturally these which the winemaker prefers to use. From the foregoing it will be seen that the role of the yeast is an important one and we can therefore formulate our first principle:

1. *Always use the best possible yeast.*

To say that yeast "feeds" upon the sugar is really an oversimplification, for what is happening is that the yeast seeks like any other form of plant or animal life to reproduce itself. For that, again like other forms of life, it must have food, oxygen and a certain degree of warmth.

Its two principal needs are sugar and oxygen. When yeast is introduced into a sugary solution which is in contact with the air it immediately starts to reproduce itself, so that the number of yeast cells in the liquid multiply extremely rapidly. This occurs during the primary, or aerobic fermentation (aerobic simply means "in contact with the air"). If the yeast were allowed to continue fermenting the liquid in this way the result would be that large quantities of yeast would be bred but the quantity of alcohol made as a by-product of the process would be small. In addition there would be the danger that the liquid might become infected by other airborne yeasts or bacteria.

When, therefore, sufficient yeast has been grown to carry through the fermentation satisfactorily, the winemaker cuts off the supply of oxygen to the yeast by employing an air-lock or fermentation trap of some sort for the whole of the secondary, or *anaerobic* (out of contact with air) fermentation. The effect of this is to force the yeast to turn to the sugar as a secondary source of oxygen, and it is this which produces the greater quantity of alcohol. The fermentation trap also protects the brew from air-borne infection and from contact with the vinegar fly.

The fermentation trap or air-lock—of which more later—is most important to the modern winemaker and gives his wine a measure of protection which was missing in days gone by.

The primary fermentation is usually quick and vigorous and may last only 3 or 4 days; the secondary fermentation will often be slow, cloudy and sometimes barely discernible; it may go on for months. The first, however, merges imperceptibly into the second and there is no clear division between the two; it is up to you to decide when to insert a fermentation trap and it is wise to do so as soon as it is safely possible without running the risk of the fermenting liquid foaming up through the trap. From this we can formulate our second principle:

2. *In order to exclude air always use an air-lock during the secondary fermentation and always keep all jars, bottles and casks as full as possible and closely covered.*

Since it is the yeast rather than ourselves which can lay claim to the litle "winemaker" it follows that to produce the best possible results we must constantly study the yeast's needs in order to give the best possible conditions in which to thrive. Just as plants need the right type of soil and the right fertilizer to flourish to the best advantage, so the yeast needs the same care.

In the solution in which it is growing—and even yeast will not grow in a sugary solution alone—it will need, in addition to oxygen and the right amount of sugar, certain nutrients, mainly nitrogenous matter and proteins, and if these are not present they must be introduced. If the nutrient *is* present the yeast will carry the fermentation further and you will have a stronger and sounder wine, with less risk of a quantity of unused sugar being left in the solution to make your finished wine very sweet. A certain amount of acid is also needed to prevent bacteria from spoiling the finished wine and to avoid its having an unpleasant medicinal laste. Also desirable is the presence of some tannin to give the necessary astringency or "bite".

"Must" made from grapes, whether pulp or juice, is an ideal medium for the yeast. In well-ripened grapes all these essential ingredients are present naturally. The sugar is there and in roughly the right quantity (too much sugar is as great an obstacle to yeast as too little). The nutrient is there, so is the acid and so is the tannin, but even with grape juice it will often be necessary to make some adjustment to one or other of these.

We who make country wine, however, are concerned not merely with grape juice, but with flavoured liquids obtained from all sorts of sources—fruit, berries, roots, grains, leaves, sap and flowers among them. We are, therefore, likely to encounter many more deficiencies than the vintner working only with grapes. Flower wines, for instance, are obviously deficient in the nutrient which the yeast demands. Some fruit will be far too acid, others will not be acid enough and many of the flower and fruit wines will require added tannin. The biggest deficiency of all, since we heavily dilute many of the juices, will be in sugar, and we may have to add up to 3 lbs. of sugar to the Imperial gallon in order to produce even a dry wine.

The whole secret of a good recipe is that its instructions are such that they produce a "must" which is in balance and gives the yeast the best possible chance to produce a good result as well as a pleasant flavour.

Here, then, we have our third and fourth principles:

3. *Always ensure that your "must" is well balanced in essentials. Be sure to include, in particular, sufficient acid.*

4. *Always use a good yeast nutrient to boost the action of your yeast.*

While the fermentation is in progress the liquid will be milky or cloudy, so much so that you will wonder whether it will ever become a really clear wine. As the secondary fermentation proceeds towards completion, the wine will slowly start to clear from the top downwards. When this occurs the wine must be "racked" or siphoned off the yeast deposit, a process which should be repeated once or twice subsequently as the deposit accumulates. This will help not only to clear the wine but also to stabilize it or bring it to the state in which it can be safely bottled. The wine is said to be unstable when fermentation is not really finished.

Most beginners make the mistake of bottling their wine *far* too soon with the result that the fermentation continues imperceptibly in the bottle until such a pressure is built up that the bottle explodes, sometimes with disastrous results. Adequate "racking", then, will vastly improve the quality of your wine, help to clear it and help to stabilize it. Moreover, if wine is left standing on a deposit of dead yeast it will acquire a distinct "off" flavour. The fifth and sixth principles are therefore:

5. *Always rack your wine from the lees as soon as fermentation is finished.*

6. *Do not be impatient to bottle.*

Normally, well-made wine will clear of its own accord given adequate time, but if it does not, it may be necessary to filter it, or to "fine" it, but we would suggest that these be regarded as emergency measures rather than routine ones. In other words:

7. *Filter or use "finings"—only if unavoidable.*

Few chemicals are necessary in winemaking, and many winemakers deplore their use at all, but one is virtually indispensable—sulphite, in one form or another. Its value lies in the fact that it is a valuable purifying or sterilizing agent, and as such it can be used for suppressing unwanted "wild" yeasts, which may be present on fruit or in fruit juice and hence in the 'must". It will also stop a fermentation permanently when desired, and is used for sterilizing all containers and equipment, for preventing the oxidation of wines, and for making a sterilizing solution for use in the U-bend of the fermentation trap.

The many uses of sulphite will be dealt with fully in a later chapter and here it will be sufficient to note that either potassium metabisulphite or sodium metabisulphite can be used. For winemaking purposes they are interchangeable. The most handy form in which the chemical can be purchased is as Campden tablets—ordinary fruit preserving tablets, which each contain 7 grains (or nearly half a gram) of metabisulphite.

One tablet should be added to each gallon or 5 litres of liquid to be fermented 24 hrs. before the chosen yeast is introduced. It will kill or inhibit wild and unwanted yeasts, but by the time the selected yeast is added its action will have diminished sufficiently for the vigorously fermenting fresh yeast not be affected and this will proceed with its work unhindered.

It is unnecessary, of course, to sulphite a "must" in which boiling water has been used, or when the ingredients have been boiled, since any wild yeast present will in that case already have been killed. But keep a supply of these useful tablets by you, or a stock solution of the chemical, and remember:

> 8. *If you have not otherwise purified your "must", always sulphite 24 hrs. before introducing your chosen yeast.*

Many winemakers run into the difficulty that their finished wines are so over-sweet as to be syrupy and undrinkable. This is often the fault of old recipes which recommend the use of too much sugar (on the principle of one more for the pot, we suspect!). Over-sweet wines can be avoided by the use of a good nutrient to enable the yeast to work with the maximum efficiency, and by not using too much sugar initially. There is little that one can do with an over-sweet wine, whereas a dry wine can always be sweetened to taste. As another principle, therefore, we would suggest:

> 9. *Avoid over-sweet wine by using only sufficient sugar to produce a dry wine of the strength you require and then sweeten it to taste when finished.*

Since the juices with which you are working will often contain natural sugar in varying amounts, how are we to calculate how much sugar to add so as to be sure not to produce an over-sweet wine? It is here that that useful instrument, the hydrometer, proves its worth. As will be explained in Chapter 9, by using the hydrometer we can measure the sugar content of a liquid and also calculate how much extra sugar will be needed to produce a wine of any required strength. It will also enable us to calculate the exact strength of our finished wine. So:

> 10. *Use your hydrometer regularly for all three purposes.*

Finally and perhaps most important of all, as will be explained later, always take the utmost precautions to protect your wine from the attentions of your worst enemy, the vinegar fly, or it will turn to a curiously flavoured vinegar. Do this by:

11. *Making sure that any ferment in an open "crock" or other similar container is always closely covered by two or three thicknesses of cloth or a sheet of polyethylene secured with a rubber band, and by using a fermentation lock wherever possible.*

THIS IS SO IMPORTANT THAT IT CANNOT BE OVER-
EMPHASIZED.

Chapter 4

THE MAIN INGREDIENTS: I. YEAST

HAVING SAID something about the principles involved in the making of wine, let us take a closer look at the main "ingredients"—yeast, flavour, sugar, acidity, nutrient, tannin, water and time, the time required for maturation (often the most difficult of the eight to allow in sufficient quantity).

The word "yeast" to most people conjures up a mental image of a lump of the soft, brown substance that one purchased at the baker's, and indeed many old wine books specify simply in their recipes "one ounce of baker's yeast", often "spread on a slice of toast".

It is understandable that this type of yeast should be the most widely known, for firstly it used to be readily available, very cheaply, almost everywhere, and it was natural, when every household did its own baking and brewing, that the two processes should be carried on side by side and the same yeast utilized for both.

But there are literally hundreds of yeasts, all with their own inherent and often subtle characteristics and all clearly discernible—under a microscope or by their behaviour—as being different, often widely so. There are thus yeasts suitable for baking, there are yeasts suitable for brewing, there are yeasts suitable for winemaking, there are non-fermenting yeasts, there are top fermenting yeasts, often used in brewing, and bottom fermenting yeasts, preferred in winemaking; there are even yeasts which have a pathogenic role and can cause disease.

Under a microscope, for instance, the cells of baker's yeast *(Saccharomyces cerevisiae)* are seen to be mainly spherical, whereas the two yeasts commonly encountered in winemaking —wild yeast *(saccharomyces apiculatus)* and wine yeast *(saccharomyces ellipsoideus)*—have mainly lemon-shapped and oval cells respectively.

Saccharomyces simply means "sugar fungi", for yeast is classified as a plant. In certain circumstances many yeasts form spores, like the seed of any other plant. This spore can withstand extremes of temperature and remain dormant but alive for many years, until in a suitable environment it is rehabilitated. Yeast cells are invisible to the naked eye, but can be seen clearly under a microscope when magnified 500 to 1,000 times. If you could lay the cells side by side 5,000 would only measure 1 in. Professor Cruess, the American oenologist, reckons that there are 6,000 million yeast cells in 1 fluid oz. or 30 ml. of an actively

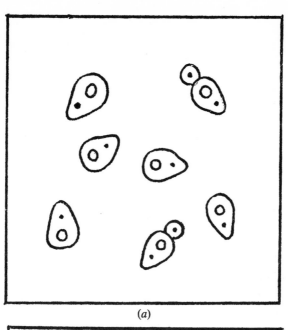

(a)

(b)

Fig 11   Yeast cells, magnified 1,000 times.
(a) Saccharomyces ellipsoideus (wine yeast)
(b) Saccharomyces apiculatus (wild yeast)

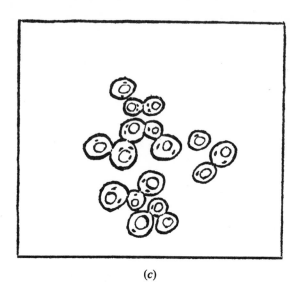

(c)

Fig 11 (c) Saccharomyces cerevisiae (bakers' yeast

fermenting wine must. For the technically minded, a fully grown *saccharomyces ellipsoideus* cell measures according to Rahn 7·2 × 5·6 *u*. (*u* is one millionth of a meter.)

The story of yeast is a fascinating one. Much of our modern knowledge stems from the work of the great scientist Louis Pasteur, who did much original work on the subject almost exactly a century ago—research which, in the hands of his successors, reached its culmination only a decade or so ago. The complicated chemistry of the whole process of fermentation has now been broken down into its various stages.

Before Pasteur's discoveries, however, scientific belief was the opposite to what it is today, for in those times people though that fermentation and putrefaction were the crucible of living organisms and that life was created by a fermentation instead of being the cause of it. This was known as the theory of "spontaneous generation" and Pasteur had a long and uphill struggle convincing other scientists of the simple fact that microorganisms such as yeast could and did cause certain chemical changes.

Pasteur reasoned that yeast needed oxygen in order to live, that it obtained this oxygen from the fermentable material and that in so doing it caused the breakdown of sugar. This was not exactly correct, but it was this reasoning that formed the basis of subsequent research and it was only as recently as 1942 that Meyerhof proved that the essential with which fermentation provided the yeast was not oxygen but energy.

It had also been discovered some 45 years earlier that it was not yeast itself which was the true fermentation agent but substances in yeast called enzymes. One yeast cell may contain a thousand different enzymes, an enzyme being a catalyst or a substance which has the power to bring about a change without undergoing any changes itself.

Thus it was discovered that yeast respires, or breathes, in much the same way as we do. It takes in oxygen and expires carbon dioxide. And just as man takes in food as fuel and from it produces the energy he needs for warmth, movement and certain internal chemical changes, so yeast takes in oxygen and produces energy; energy which is devoted not to locomotion but to self-reproduction.

If we prevent any form of life from respiring—i.e. if we cut off its oxygen supply—the plant or animal dies, but here yeast has the advantage! If we cut off *its* oxygen supply it has a secondary method by which it can obtain the energy it needs for self-reproduction. It obtains that energy mainly from the sugar which is present in the liquid and it is this which gives us the type of fermentation we need, high in attenuation, or in other words alcohol formation. The two main products are alcohol and carbon dioxide, in roughly equal parts by weight. This is shown in the chemical equation:

$$C_6H_{12}O_6 \rightarrow 2C_2H_5OH + 2CO_2$$

i.e. one molecule of sugar (fruit sugar is shown in the equation) is changed into two molecules of alcohol plus two molecules of carbon dioxide.

The principal yeast growth, it should be noted, occurs during the aerobic ferment; once the oxygen is cut off the yeast multiplies much more slowly but produces more alcohol. That is why we use the air-lock in order to bring about this result. When the concentration of alcohol is sufficient, usually somewhere about 15% by volume, the yeast is inhibited from further activity.

As we have said, there are many hundreds of types of yeast, and they are all about us. These tiny micro-organisms are to be found in the bloom on grapes or other fruit, in the air, in the soil, on flowers, in pollen and even in our mouths. They are, in fact, almost ubiquitous. The various kinds have been given Latin names in botanical fashion and under a microscope their different characteristics can be recognized, though sometimes only by stimulating them to form spores which are fundamentally different for each variety. Some have round cells, some elliptical, some triangular, and they have different methods of reproduction. In some cases the main yeast cell grows a "bud" which eventually become a cell in its own right. In others the main cell "gives birth" to a daughter cell and in yet another reproduction is achieved by the fission of a single cell; the cell just splits into two. Yeasts even have a sex life of their own. There are male and female strains which can fuse together to produce 'young"' which can repeat the process.

Of all these hundreds of yeasts, baker's yeast may be the most familiar, but modern winemakers know that it is by no means ideal for their purpose. In bakery what is required is a yeast that will act quickly and vigorously to produce the gaseousness required to make the loaf or cake mixture "rise"; much the same action is demanded of beer yeast. What is required of a wine yeast, however, is completely different. Here we need a quiet, slow ferment, which will leave unimpaired, or even improved, the suble flavours we seek; and above all we need a yeast which will be able to survive as high a concentration of alcohol as possible before it finally succumbs—i.e. one that has a high alcohol tolerance.

Scientists, chiefly in the wine-producing countries, have devoted years of research to discovering and culturing such yeasts, which are thus rightly called "selected wine yeasts". These are the yeasts which the modern amateur winemaker is now able to use. They give him a stronger wine, with its bouquet and flavour unimpaired.

Baker's yeast will normally succumb at 14% to 15% alcohol, but wine yeasts will carry a fermentation to 16% or 17% and some suppliers claim that it will attain as much as 20%.

Wine yeasts also give a firmer sediment which, since it is less easily disturbed, will make "racking" less troublesome. Above all, they will give the slow, steady fermentation which is required for wine.

The first time you use a wine yeast you may be a little disappointed. Gone is the vigorous, frothy ferment to which you have been accustomed and at times the only sign of fermentation will be the tiny bubbles rising to the surface round the circumference of the liquor. But do not worry, this is as it should be and a better wine will result.

Baker's yeast is cheap, and will ferment at a comparatively low temperature. It is often far more vigorous than a true wine yeast, giving a frothy and "showy" fermentation in the first instance. This is often encouraging to the beginner who may well like to use a baker's yeast for the first few wines put down.

Baker's yeast can be added direct to the liquid and it is best to use not more than ½ oz. per gallon or 15 grams per 5 litres or you will have an overheavy deposit of yeast. The same applies to brewer's yeast, which is ideal for beers and ales but which is apt to impart a beery flavour to the wine. You will notice that it has a distinct beer odour even before being added to the brew.

Granulated yeast which is sold in packets by food stores, is another form of baker's yeast. Use only a level teaspoonful to the gallon. This is ample and there is no need to increase the amount given here in direct proportion for making more than 1 gal. With all baker's yeasts racking is even more important than with wine yeast. If the wine is left standing on the less you will definitely have "off" flavours and a musty odour which is instantly detectable.

Wine Yeast. Gradually, all winemakers come to realize that there are better things to be had and will set out in search of that elusive thing—quality. Inevitably, the first improvement is to use a true wine yeast suitable for the type of wine that it is intended to make, a port or Burgundy yeast for a red wine such as elderberry or blackberry; a sherry or Sauterne yeast for elderflower, apple or similar wine; a Champagne yeast for sparkling wine, and a lager or brewer's yeast for experimenting with beers.

Wine yeasts can be obtained in several forms: as a culture growing upon a sliver of agar jelly in a test-tube, in liquid form or in powder or tablet form. They need a little more care in preparation and usually, since they come from sunnier climes, will require a slightly higher temperature initially. The results will be found to be well worth the extra trouble.

Since these yeasts have had to be cultured and specially prepared they are also more expensive than baker's yeast, but it is often overlooked that they can be made to last for the whole of a winemaking season, since the user can propagate his own culture once he has purchased the initial quantity, and can also use the deposit from previous ferments to start subsequent wines.

A wine yeast must be activated before being added to the bulk of the liquid, for the quantity suppied may be very small. Activation means that the yeast must be brought to the state of active fermentation in some sterilized fruit juice, which contains all the nutrients needed. Care should also be taken that this is done in sterilized conditions to prevent the new yeast from becoming infected by any others, either airborne or in the ingredients.

The yeast should be activated in a "starter bottle"—any 1-pt. (½ litre) bottle will do—some 48 hrs. at least before it will be wanted, so that when you come to make your wine the starter bottle is in full ferment and the yeast thus has a much better chance of success.

For the starter juice one can use either the juice from which the wine is to be made (if some can be obtained beforehand) or some other fruit juice. You need only ½ pt. or so of it and the flavour of the wine will not be affected. To this add 1 oz. (30 grams) of sugar. Or you can use a tablespoonful of pure malt extract, a tablespoonful of granulated sugar, the juice of a lemon and ½ pt. (300 ml.) of water. (See also the section on nutrients.) Whatever you use, bring it to the boil in an aluminium or sound enamel saucepan to sterilize it, and then allow it to cool.

To activate a tube culture, first sterilize a small bottle by boiling it in water for 5 mins.' allow it to cool, and plug it with clean cotton wool. Stand the tube culture in warm (*not* boiling) water for a few minutes to loosen the agar, or jelly, which bears the yeast culture, and then, with a knitting needle or some such instrument which has been dipped in boiling water, coax the agar, and with it the yeast, into the bottle. Pour in the prepared starter juice, plugging the neck of the bottle with cotton wool and standing it in a temperature of about 70° F (21° C).

After 2 to 3 days the starter bottle will be in full ferment and tiny bubbles will be seen rising to the surface. It can then be added to the bulk of the liquid. This will suffice for 1 to 3 gals.

A bottle culture is a little handier, for the bottle juice has

Fig 12   Starter bottle

merely to be poured into the yeast bottle and the cotton wool replaced. After 24 hrs. in a warm place fermentation will be under way, and after a few days there will be enough yeast to start from 5 to 10 gals. of must. If you wish to use a starter bottle at intervals through the season for successive brews it is as well to make up a starter juice from ½ cup of orange and ¼ cup of lemon juice—preferably strained—plus ½ cup of water and 1 oz. (30 grams) of sugar. When the yeast has been added and has begun to ferment, three-quarters of it can be used to activate a must and the remaining quarter can be topped up with juice made up as before. After a week or so this new starter will also be fermenting and will be ready for use again. The process can be repeated *ad infinitum*. This process can be applied, of course, to any wine yeast culture and is a very worthwhile procedure.

The yeast which is thrown out as a sediment during fermentation can also be used to ferment subsequent liquor, but it should be noted that it is wiser to use lees from the *second* racking rather than those from the first, which are liable to contain too many unwanted substances other than yeast.

The yeast from the *second* racking, on the other hand, is almost a pure wine yeast and it is a pity to waste it. It can be activated, if necessary, as above. Such yeast can be conserved by pouring it on blotting paper to dry it slowly and by keeping it in a sterile, screw-top jar until required, when it is activated in the usual way. Only yeast from a wine which is still in course of fermentation, or which has just finished fermenting, should be used, for any lees from a wine made long since will have autolyzed and will be dead.

Yeast sold in tablet or in powder form has also to be activated, but individual suppliers send detailed instructions with their products and you will find the process quite simple.

Finally, a word of warning about "no yeast" recipes. There is no such thing! If a ferment occurs it can only be because yeast is present; therefore if you use a recipe which omits all mention of yeast, it does not mean that no yeast is being used but merely that you are relying on any wild yeast that may be present on the fruit or other ingredients. This *may* work, but far more likely it will go dreadfully wrong: you are taking a very doubtful chance.

Even when working in grapes, European vignerons first sulphite the must to kill the wild yeasts and bacteria; subsequently they introduce their selected wine yeasts. They know that in this way their chances of success are immeasurably greater: you will be well advised do do the same.

Chapter 5

THE MAIN INGREDIENTS: II. FLAVOUR

A S WINEMAKERS we are fortunate in that we have a really wide range of basic flavours at our disposal—the fruits of our gardens and countryside are ours to command, and soft and hard fruit, vegetables, flowers, berries, grain, herbs, leaves, tendrils and sap, can be pressed into service. And even these flavours can be further extended by modification of basic recipes, and by the addition of flavourings, spices and other ingredients.

There are really only two main ways of extracting flavour, and they might be described broadly as the juice and the pulp methods.

Pressing or a commercial fruit juice extractor is employed for the juice method, and really needs little explanation, for it consists simply of expressing the juice from a fruit. It is naturally suitable for any soft fruit with a high juice content, but unsuitable for roots, grain, flowers or similar ingredients. This is the method employed for white wine from grapes. The juice being thus separated from the pulp, diluted, adjusted and sugared as necessary, can then be fermented immediately. The great advantage of this method is that the must can go into a fermenting vessel and under an air-lock without delay and the consequent risk of infection. It is not really so difficult to obtain or contrive some form of press (see Chapter 29) and this method can be adapted and used for a wide range of wines and other drinks—apple, elderberry, blackberry, pear, orange, grape, cider and so on.

The pulp method can take several forms. The ferment may either be started as soon as the fruit has been mashed and before the liquid has been strained off, or the flavour may first be extracted by boiling the ingredients, or simply by steeping them in water for a few days. The water in some recipes will be cold, in others it will be poured on when boiling. Let us look at each of these methods in a little more detail.

Fermenting on the pulp. The fruit is cut up or crushed, water and sulphite are added and then, 24 hrs. later, yeast is also added. The ferment is allowed to proceed for up to 10 days (sugar being added if necessary) before the liquid is strained off the pulp, further sugared, poured into a fermenting jar, and a trap fitted. Because of the bulk of the ingredients a large vessel such as a crock, closely covered, will often have to be used for the first stage. This method is the one used for red wine from grapes, since the colour of the skins passes into the wine. It is likewise employed with some fruit wines where colour extraction is important, or where the juice content may be comparatively small. It is useful for apple, plum, blackberry, cherry and similar wines.

Boiling is self-explanatory. The main ingredient is boiled in the water—or in as much of it as may be necessary—for such time as it will take to extract the flavour. It is the method most commonly used with roots such as parsnip. It is one which has to be used with great care since over-boiling will usually result in a wine which later will fail to clear, or will be subject to peculiar coloured hazes. The reason for this is that pectins (gummy substances) are released by the boiling, which kills an enzyme which would otherwise destroy them. If present in large quantities pectins will jellify in the wine later. See also the chapter on Ailments of Wine.

Care should therefore always be taken that roots are not boiled so long that they become "mushy", or this trouble will occur, and it is one which is quite difficult to correct. Boiling water, on the other hand, is extremely useful in that it will kill any unwanted wild yeast or bacteria which may be present on the main ingredients, thus obviating the need to use sulphite.

Steeping in either hot or cold water is used for a wide range of wines, especially those made from grain. Pour the boiling water over the ingredients, cover the crock closely and then leave them to soak from 3 to 10 days. This is, of course, really using the same method as we employ when we make a pot of tea—we are infusing. This method has the double merit that the boiling water not only extracts the flavour but also purifies the must, and without the dangers consequent upon over-boiling. Here, then, is the best of both worlds. Subsequently the liquid is strained off the must and fermented in the usual way. Many recipes recommend periods of steeping which are overlong and unnecessary, sometimes as much as three weeks. After ten days or so all the flavour possible has in fact been extracted, and if you prolong the period you are merely inviting infection and accomplishing nothing.

It is important in all these wines which involve steeping that the must be stirred, at least once, and preferably twice, a day; it can hardly be overdone. But keep the crock well covered.

Before making a grain wine it is a good idea to soak the grain in a little water overnight, then to run it through a mincer together with the raisins. This will make doubly sure that 10 days are ample time for steeping and it will be quite unnecessary to soak the grain for 3 weeks.

Chapter 6

THE MAIN INGREDIENTS: III. SUGAR

SUGAR, IN the form of sugar cane, originated in Java and South-East Asia and it reached Europe by way of China, India and Persia.

The first known· reference to it is in a Hindu book written about 500 B.C., but more information was given about 300 B.C. by Nearchus, who reported to Alexander the Great that he had seen "reeds that produced honey, although there were no bees".

At first, however, sugar was so rare and expensive that it was the food only of kings and the very wealthy. The first importation of sugar into England was in 1624 when King Henry III ordered sugar for the Royal Household. The equivalent cost today would be $25 a pound. Other people used honey as their main sweetening agent—hence the popularity in those days of mead as a fermented drink. In 1942 Columbus took the plant to the New World and so started the great West Indian sugar plantations.

The first sugar refinery was started in England as early as 1544, but it was not until the middle of the eighteenth century, with the opening up of the West Indies (plus the use of slave labour)· that the price was sufficiently reduced to make sugar available to all.

There are several types of sugar and the winemaker is not always quite clear as to what they are, as to the relationship between them, and as to their respective advantages and disadvantages. There is no space here to deal with all forms of sugar or to delve deeply into complicated chemistry, but the few principal sugars that the winemaker is likely to encounter will be discussed in general.

All modern white, refined sugars have a high level of purity and whether cane, beet, preserving or invert, they can all safely be used in any wine. The principal types of sugar are:

Glucose (or grape sugar), which is found abundantly in most sweet fruits. It is the ideal sugar for fermentation, since it can be changed in one stage of enzymatic action directly into alcohol and carbon dioxide, the enzyme which performs this useful function being zymase. Glucose is only about half as sweet as sucrose, the next sugar to be discussed. Nevertheless, it is used in brewing and in the manufacture of caramel. It is also used in making confectionery and as a raw material for several products within the food industry. Pure glucose can be purchased for use in winemaking but is somewhat expensive.

Sucrose (or cane sugar) is the ordinary sweetener used in the home, in industry and by the majority of winemakers. This is not a simple sugar chemically, but a combination of two—glucose and fructose. The action of another enzyme in the yeast called "invertase" splits the sucrose into its two components and is said to "invert" the sugar. The succeeding chemical changes by zymase again produce alcohol and carbon dioxide.

Beet and *Cane* Sugar are chemically the same substance— sucrose—but each contains minute impurities and in fact, therefore, they are not completely the same. It is these impurities which may account for any difference in result when making wine. For reasons not easy to define most winemakers prefer cane sugar. We think that it may well be superior to beet sugar, although a chemist might pooh-pooh the idea!

Beet sugar, incidentally, was one of the few good things to come out of the Napoleonic wars. Cut off from France's source of sugar in the New World, Napoleon set his scientists and agriculturalists the task of finding another source—and that was the start of the sugar beet industry, which has now spread all over Europe. Every country today likes to feel that, should war come, it still has its own source of sugar at home.

Both cane and beet sugar are easily fermented and because of their ready availability and cheapness are likely to remain for some time the principal, if not necessarily the best, sugar winemakers use. They do not noticeably alter flavour and, therefore, can safely be used in any wine, however delicate.

The sucrose in everyday use takes many forms and a refinery will produce it in 24 or 25 different guises—from fine crystals to coloured fancy sugars, from Demerara to cube sugar.

Preserving Sugar is preferable in making jams or preserves because of its porosity and because it will not settle hard on the bottom of the pan as quickly as other sugars. But it has no advantage over ordinary household sugar for winemaking.

"Burnt Sugar", a phrase encountered in some old winemaking books, is only a poetic name for what is known in the trade as *Caramel*. There are now many commercial grades developed for specific purposes and given numbers for identification. They have little use in winemaking (other than for colouring beers, etc.) because they will usually impart a flavour.

"Pieces" is a name given to sugar which is a by-product of the refinery, and which is used for certain industrial purposes and in brewing. Its main advantage is that it dissolves rapidly. It is not likely to be of particular use to the winemaker.

Demerara, an original raw sugar with a large grain size which has not been filtered, and *Brown* sugar have only one real advantage to the winemaker, they both impart a golden colour to what might perhaps be an otherwise uninteresting-looking wine. But they may also give a flavour which can overlay the main one. Their use should consequently be restricted to occasions when one or both of these results is desired. With a delicate wine their use should certainly be avoided. Even further down the scale come *Black Treacle* and *Molasses,* which are very strongly flavoured. These are best only used in home-brewed stouts.

Candy Sugar is specified in many old recipes but this is because those recipes are traditional and because it was once the purest form of sugar one could purchase. With the advent of modern refined sugar this is no longer true and candy sugar has no advantage.

Invert Sugar (see Sucrose) is a mixture and not a combination of glucose and fructose. It is produced by the hydrolysis of cane sugar, of varying degrees of refinement, by sulphuric or hydrochloric acid, followed by neutralization, concentration, removal of mineral salts, and filtration. The hydrolysis is similar to that effected by yeast, which produces roughly equal amounts of glucose and fructose.

Invert sugar is used commercially for beer making and ferments out quickly and completely. It can now be bought by the amateur winemaker and its use should enable the fermentation to go smoothy and resemble that of grape juice, which is noticeably quicker to ferment than most of our country wines. Invert, however, is more than twice as expensive as domestic sugar but it can be made simply by boiling the sugar with 1 tsp. of citric acid in water for 20 minutes.

Fructose (or Laevulose) is very sweet, sweeter than cane sugar, and is found, with glucose, in sweet fruits, leaves and flowers. *Honey* is a mixture of fructose, glucose and sometimes sucrose. Fructose is easily fermented.

Maltose is a rather complicated form of sugar produced from starches. Yeast cannot act upon starches, which are rather like sugars, unless they are first malted. In malting, an enzyme—diastase—found in malt and germinating seeds, changes starch into maltose. Then another enzyme in the yeast turns maltose into a simple sugar and the fermentation proceeds.

In Bavaria only beer made with malt is recognized as beer—no sugar addition is allowed—but with malt the price it is, the home brewer, like the commercial brewer in this country, can hardly afford this practice. He will add sugar to his liquor and in that way will be able to make it stronger and more cheaply.

Lactose (milk sugar) is one of which we hear little and reference to it in the wine sections of this book is perhaps a little academic. It contains glucose and galactose and only certain yeasts will ferment it. It cannot be fermented by saccharomyces ellipsoideus or cerevisiae, for example. It is sometimes added to a stout beer to make "milk stout".

Starch, of course, is a source of sugar, and glucose can be obtained by boiling starches in dilute mineral acid, but the starches found in cereals, beet and potatoes are associated with proteins, which, on fermentation, produce *fusel oil*. This is not to say that small quantities of these ingredients cannot be used in a recipe for flavouring purposes, but merely that one would be ill-advised to attempt to produce *all* the sugar one needed in this way. Starch fermentation to produce sugar is full of danger for the amateur and quite unnecessary· since sugar is plentiful and cheap.

Many old recipes suggest the use of far too much sugar, often as much as 4½ lbs. to 1 gal. (2¼ kg. to 5 litres) of must. There are exceptions, of course, but generally the effect of this will be to produce a wine which is horribly over-sweet. What happens is that the yeast finds it almost as difficult to cope with too much sugar as with not enough; it is rather like a plant being over-manured or given a double dose of concentrated fertilizer. The yeast fails to convert sufficient sugar and the balance is left sweetening the wine, which is therefore too sweet.

If you are not using a hydrometer and are working by rule of thumb, bear in mind the figure 3 lbs. to the Imperial gallon, 2½ lb. per U.S. gallon, 1½ Kilo per 5 litres: put ½ lb. (250 g.) less for a dry wine and ½ lb. more for a sweet one. You will find it better, as a rule, to make a dry wine and then to sweeten it finally to your taste, than to endeavour to put into your must at the outset all the sugar that you think you will require to produce a wine of a certain sweetness.

It is much better, then, not to add at the outset all the sugar which you calculate you will require in a particular wine.

It is far preferable to add, say, half the sugar to start with and then, when the fermentation is going well, to add the remainder in 4-oz. (125 g.) lots by stages, each time the ferment begins to slow. At first, of course, the sugar will be consumed quickly, but as the ferment progresses the rate of sugar consumption will drop and the additions will be ever more widely spaced. If you are not using a hydrometer this can only be checked visually by the speed with which bubbles are passing through the fermentation trap, or by taste, as the wine reaches dryness as each successive addition of sugar is consumed.

If you are using a hydrometer, you have a much more accurate guide to the speed of the ferment in the successive drops in specific gravity, and this is fully dealt with in our chapter on the hydrometer.

When adding solid sugar to a wine it is not really advisable to do so directly to the bulk of the fermenting wine, for if it is not all dissolved it may cause the ferment to "stick", or temporarily cease. It is better to siphon off half a pint of the wine and to dissolve the small amount of sugar in this (without using heat, of course, which would kill the yeast present). Stir thoroughly and make sure that all the sugar is completely dissolved before returning this small quantity of sweetened wine to the bulk.

Another occasion when the use of sugar will be necessary is when you need to "top up", to replace any wastage in order to keep a fermenting vessel full to exclude all air. This can be done with syrup (i.e. sugar dissolved in boiled water) of the same strength as the original must.

Chapter 7

THE MAIN INGREDIENTS: IV. ACIDITY

INSUFFICIENT ACID in a wine during the making does result in a most unpleasant medicinal taste in the finished product which is quite distinctive, and it is imperative, therefore, to see that enough acid—but not too much—is included in the must.

In grape juice severals acids are found—tartaric, malic (called thus because it is found in apples), citric, lactic (the acid found in sour milk), and succinic, the last two being of minor importance. Tartaric acid, up to two parts per thousand, is useful in that it helps in producing a sound wine which will keep, but above about twelve parts per thousand it gives the wine a tart taste.

Even with grapes the acid content can vary widely, as much as 2%, and European vignerons, therefore, find it necessary to test and adjust their must. How much more desirable, then, is it for us to do the same, dealing as we do with a much more extensive range of ingredients, with a wider variation of acid content.

Where the juice is too acid we need to reduce the acidity, and where it is not acid enough, or totally lacking in acid, we have to add some, usually in the form of citric acid. This is preferable to tartaric, which may cause hazes in the finished wine.

Generally speaking, it is desirable that a must should have an acid content of between ½% and ¾%. This is equivalent to the juice of four to six large lemons, or four level teaspoons of citric acid per gallon of must.

This is the amount which would have to be added, it should be emphasized, if one had a completely neutral juice: but some acid will usually be present naturally.

With many fruit juices, the dilution with water specified in the recipe will be sufficient to reduce the acidity to a reasonable level, and that is why in most cases the country winemaker practises dilution; recipes are designed with this in mind.

Usually 4 to 6 lbs. of fruit to the Imperial gallon of water will produce a juice which is roughly right in acid content, but there can be wide variations, and with certain over-acid and under-acid ingredients special care is demanded.

It is not easy to give a simple but accurate picture of the acidity of our principal ingredients, since a far wider range is to be found in some fruits than in others. Some fruits range from 1·5% to 3%, some from 0·5% to 2·5%, while others may have a variation of only about 0.5%.

Taking their generally found acidities, however, one could group them, and the treatment required, roughly like this:

Acid Content	Fruit	Treatment per gal. (5 l.)
1. Very high.	Rhubarb; red, white and black currants.	Remove some acid with precipitated chalk.
2. High.	Cherries; raspberries; gooseberries.	Dilute slightly more than usual.
3. Medium.	Grapes; strawberries; blackberries; apples; plums.	Add the juice of one lemon.
4. Low.	Flower wines; raisin and dried fruit.	Add the juice of 2 lemons or ¼ oz. citric acid (one heaped teaspoon).
5. Very low or deficient.	Figs; dates; vegetables; cereals.	Add the juice of 4–6 lemons or ½–¾ oz. citric acid (four level teaspoons).

In the first category it is often not possible to reduce the acidity sufficiently by dilution since the wine would have no "body" and little flavour, so great would be the dilution required.

Therefore, in the case of rhubarb (which contains oxalic acid, harmful if drunk in large quantities) and currants we often resort to reducing the acidity by means of precipitated chalk (as described in "Preparing the Must", Chapter 12). It *may* be possible to remove some of the acid, leaving just sufficient in the wine, but it is normally more practical (and in the case of rhubarb desirable) to remove *all* the acid and then add the right quantity of citric acid. If the juice has been considerably diluted, the addition of ½—1lb. grain (barley or wheat) will often add body to the wine, but it will, of course, change the flavour slightly.

Juices high in acid (No. 2) can usually be dealt with satisfactorily by dilution and by the employment of a little grain.

Do not fall into the trap of thinking that by adding sugar you are correcting over-acidity, even with a finished wine. It may mask the acidity to a certain extent, but will not remove it; you are merely overlaying one strong taste with another, instead of correcting the offending one, and this will not improve the quality of your wine. Far better to endeavour to remedy matters by stirring up any lees there may be in an unracked wine, in the hope of creating a malo-lactic ferment, which does reduce acidity, or to add up to 5% glycerine by volume, which has a marked effect.

Nor will adding too much sugar to the must help. Indeed, it may well inhibit the yeast from doing its work satisfactorily while the acid content will be unaffected.

The winemaker can test the acidity of his juice by means of an acid test kit—there are both expensive and comparatively cheap ones to be had.

In the popular version a graduated syringe is used to take in a given quantity of the liquid to be tested and this is run into a beaker. A few drops of phenolphthalein are added. This is an indicator: colourless in acid but turning pink in alkaline solutions. A commercially prepared solution of potassium or sodium hydroxide is then drawn into the syringe. Slowly this solution is added to the liquid already in the beaker until the solution just turns pink. At this point you note how much solution you have used and from that you can calculate, from the chart supplied, the percentage of acid in the liquid. From ½% to ¾% is adequate. For the sake of accuracy three tests should be made and the average reading should be taken. This simple version, consisting of graduated syringe, beaker, chemical solutions, chart and full instructions, can now be obtained for just over $2. A more elaborate set costs about $5.

In recent years improvements have been made on litmus papers, so that we now have graduated pH papers, which tell us approximately how much acid or alkali is present.

For the purposes of winemaking we are concerned only with the papers which indicate acidity. The indicator papers are supplied in "books" for the different acid values and for our purposes we require two books, one with a pH range of 2.5 to 4 and one with a pH range of 4 to 5.5. On the cover of each book is a colour chart graded at intervals of 0.3. An indicator paper leaf is torn out of the book and dipped in the must or wine to be tested; the leaf will change colour according to the quantities of acid present and this colour is checked with the chart on the cover of the book.

Sufficient acid is present for wine purposes if the colour reading is about pH 4; a little over or under within the limits of 3 and 5 doesn't matter. If the reading is lower than 3 then there is *too much* acid and some must be removed. If the reading is above 5 then there is *too little* acid present and some citric acid must be added until a fresh indicator paper, dipped in the liquid, registers about 4. The "Narrow Range Indicator pH Papers" may be obtained from your winemaking supplier or from a chemicals supply house. They cost about $1 for a roll of a given range, which should last you years.

If you decide that your must is too acid, from ¼ to ½ oz. of calcium carbonate—pure chalk—may be added. This is first mixed to a smooth paste with a little of the must and then stirred in. Foaming will occur at once, because when chalk combines with acids some gas is immediately given off. Remember then to allow room for this before adding chalk. The precipitate will begin to settle but takes some time and fermentation can be started and the precipitate removed with the rest of the lees at the first racking.

From the practical point of view it is better to add only ¼ oz. of chalk per Imperial gallon at first and then to check the result before adding the final ¼ oz.

Chapter 8

OTHER INGREDIENTS: NUTRIENTS, TANNIN, WATER AND TIME

S UGAR, AS has been explained, is the principal "food" of the yeast, but alone it is not enough. Yeast cells cannot grow in a pure sugar syrup, for they require other nutrients in their "diet"—notably proteins and vitamins.

Protein is obtained from the amino-acids which should be present and which supply the nitrogen that is so essential to growth. The vitamins required are of the vitamin B group (vitamin B being a complex of about twelve substances), thiamine or vitamin B_1.

Honey is particularly deficient in these substances, so that in the making of mead the use of a nutrient is essential. The use of a nutrient is also of the greatest possible help in achieving a really dry wine, with a minimum of residual sugar. You can make one up as follows:

Sufficient for 3 gals. or 15 litres of must

```
 1  oz. (30 g.) sugar
10  oz. (300 ml.) warm water
½  level leaspoon tartaric acid            ) Obtainable from any
½  level teaspoon ammonium phosphate  ) druggist
⅓  level teaspoon Marmite or a 15 mg. tablet of vitamin B₁
```

As long as some acid, preferably citric, is included in the must the tartaric acid can be omitted when making nutrient for a wine, as distinct from mead. In most recipes citric acid is included in the form of lemon juice.

Sterilize a bottle by boiling it in water and allow it to cool. Bring to the boil the sugar, water, acid and Marmite, allow to cool, and pour into the clean bottle. Then add the ammonium phosphate and shake well till it is dissolved. The bottle should be only two-thirds full and should be plugged with clean cotton wool. The nutrient can be used with a yeast starter (as described under Yeasts) or added as required to the bulk of the must purely as a nutrient.

Another nutrient recommended by the British Beekeeping Association for one Imp. gallon or 5 litres of mead is:

Tartaric acid	80 grains (5 grams)
Ammonium sulphate	60 grains (4 g.)
Magnesium sulphate	8 grains (½ g.)
Citric acid	55 grains (3½ g.)
Potassium phosphate	30 grains (2 g.)
Common salt	30 grains (2 g.)

This quantity is sufficient for two Imp. gallons of *wine* must. The tartaric acid should be omitted if the must already contains acid, either from the ingredients or from added lemon juice. If you wish to save yourself the trouble of making up your own you can also buy several excellent proprietary yeast nutrients, with which full instructions are given.

TANNIN

The two commonest faults to be found in country wines made by newcomers to the craft are over-sweetness and insipidity, in that order.

Most winemakers soon learn to avoid the over-sweetness, but many never seem to remedy the insipidity, and their wines are consistently flat and uninspiring. If they did but know, the fault is easily corrected and their wines can be vastly improved.

Tannin is the secret. It is tannin which gives the wine its bite, or astringency, and which endows it with a degree of character. Tannin, too, is one of the principal factors in ensuring keeping quality and satisfactory maturation, so the inclusion of enough of it in the must is an excellence insurance. Its absence will be detected, perhaps, only by the educated palate: the uninitiated will know simply that the wine seems rather flat, characterless, and lacking in what is called "zest".

Tannin is found on the skins of fruit—including grapes—and in the stalks and stems. Red wine from grapes, for instance, usually has sufficient tannin because the must has been fermented "on the pulp" or skins, but white wine, where only the juice has been fermented, usually needs some added. This is regular commercial practice.

Some tannin is to be found in our fruit in this country— pear skins are particularly rich in it—but generally our country wines will be all the better for having some tannin added. This can be in the form of grape tannin, which can be purchased from winemaking suppliers, or it can be added in the form of pear skin peelings or oak leaves, which can be included in the must.

Strong, over-infused tea can also be used at the rate of one tablespoonful to every Imperial gallon and this is perhaps the most convenient method.

WATER

Throughout this chapter mention has been made of water, but so far nothing has been said about the sort of water to use. In the distant past cold water drawn from a spring or well was used in the making of wine. Sometimes this water was pure and delicious, containing minute traces of natural minerals and salts in solution which were of immense value to the wine. Sometimes alas! the water was contaminated and contained many bacteria injurious to health. Fortunately these were made harmless by the alcohol formed during fermentation, even if the wine was not improved.

Today we mostly use tap water drawn from the mains in the confidence that it is at least pure. In some places the water is naturally "soft", in others it is softened to some extent at the water works, in still others it is softened in the home. This softened water is quite all right for making wines and indeed has certain advantages, especially with flower wines. It is excellent in brewing stout and suitable also for mild ales, but a harder water containing gypsum is needed for bitter ales. In hard water areas it is advisable always to boil water before using for wine-making, to remove at least some of the hardness.

Some winemakers are convinced that it is an advantage to use cold water in all recipes, mainly on the ground that flavour is not then dissipated by the heat of boiling water. We are doubtful whether the case is really proved and on balance (with some qualifications) prefer the use of boiling water. Even tap water can contain wild yeasts and by bringing the water to the boil you can be quite certain that not only is the water sterile, but also that the "must" ingredients will be sterilized too.

But why use water at all? Could not some of our soft fruits, for example, simply be pressed and the juice alone fermented? Unhappily the product would be so lacking in sugar and so high in acid that dilution and the addition of sugar would still be imperative. With many recipes water is needed to soften the hard ingredients and to leach the flavours. For various reasons then water is an important part of almost every must. But oddly enough its benefit in one direction is sometimes a disadvantage in another. For example, diluting the acid of a sour fruit also dilutes the flavour and so care must be taken to obtain a reasonable balance.

TIME

No matter how carefully you prepare your must and ferment your wine, one intangible ingredient is fundamental—*time*. It is perhaps the most difficult ingredient to handle. A year is such a long time to wait. Yet the wise use of time can make such a tremendous difference. Allow adequate time to extract the flavour and adequate time for the fermentation. Don't be in a hurry to bottle the finished wine. If it is kept under an air-lock no harm can come to it, as long as it is not kept on a heavy deposit of lees.

For a great many years experiments have been made to age wine artificially. Commercially the need is of tremendous importance. Unfortunately no certain and successful method has yet been found and there is still no alternative ingredient to time. Time is absolutely essential for the production of a mellow and mature wine. You must leave your wine long enough for nature to smooth out the raw edges, if you want to enjoy a good wine. While some light wines of 9% or 10% alcohol mature within the year, rich or heavy wines, and especially strong wines of 15% or more alcohol, need more than a year before they can give of their best. In so many brews the last bottle to be drunk proves to be the best and one wishes in vain that one had kept the others as long. Time is the essence. Don't worry the wine. Be strongminded if you wish to be thankful.

Chapter 9

THE HYDROMETER

I T IS a fair question for those who have never used a hydro-meter to ask what this has to do with making wine and why a complete chapter is being devoted to this subject. Experience has shown that one of the most frequent errors in making wine at home is the addition of far too much sugar to the must, resulting in only slightly alcoholic fruit cordials. The hydrometer enables us not only to avoid this error but also to control the kind of wine we wish to make, throughout its fermentation. By means of it we can:

(a) Calculate how much natural sugar is present in a juice or must.

(b) Decide how strong a wine that would make (i.e. the potential alcoholic content.

(c) Work out how much sugar to add to produce a wine of the strength we desire, or,

(d) Alternatively, decide what dilution is required.

(e) Keep a check on the progress of a ferment, and

(f) Calculate reasonably accurately the strength of the finished wine.

The hydrometer is a scientific instrument for measuring the "gravity" (the density or weight) of a liquid in which it is floated. By definition, "specific gravity is the weight of a certain volume of a substance as compared with the weight of the same volume of water". All the winemaker uses it for, really, is to check the amount of sugar present in the must, ferment or wine, the factor which is the basis of his principal calculations.

The hydrometer consists of a short hollow glass tube about ½ in. in diameter, weighted with lead shot or mercury and attached to a long narrow stem about ¼ in. in diameter containing a graduated scale or scales printed upon white paper. It is used in conjunction with a sample jar which is an inch or so taller than the hydrometer and about 1½ ins. in diameter, and in which it is floated in some of the liquid to be tested.

The more sugar there is in the liquid, the thicker and denser it will be, i.e. the greater its gravity will be. The better, too, it will support anything floating in it. To measure degrees of this, we need some sort of scale and a basic standard, and the obvious one to choose is that of water, which is universally available.

In the scale most commonly used, water is given the arbitrary value of 1·000.

In water, therefore, a hydrometer floats at the mark on the top of the scale, at 1·000. In liquids the density of which is

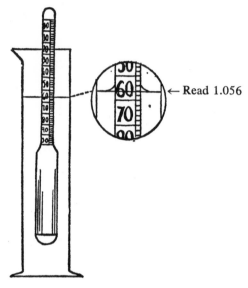

← Read 1.056

Fig 13   Hydrometer and hydrometer jar

greater than that of water, the hydrometer floats higher, and in liquids less dense than water, the hydrometer will float lower. It follows then that in a liquid containing fruit juice and sugar, which is denser than water, the hydrometer will float at a point on the scale corresponding with the quantity of sugar dissolved in the water. On the other hand if the liquid consists of wine in which all the sugar has been fermented to alcohol (which is lighter than water), then the reading will be below 1·000.

The term "Specific Gravity", strictly speaking, is applicable only to the four-figure reading; the figures after the decimal point are described as the "gravity". Thus a *specific gravity* of 1·140 is the same as a *gravity* of 140.

There are hydrometers marked in other scales, of course, notably Baumé, Brix and Twaddell, and our table below compares these with the Specific Gravity scale, and is reasonably accurate. It will be noticed, and is worth remembering, that 1 deg. Twaddell = 5 degs. Specific Gravity. The Brix scale is in percentage of sugar by weight in pure water.

Specific Gravity	Degs. Baumé	Degs. Twaddell	Degs. Brix
1·005	1·0	1·0	1·6
1·010	1·4	2·0	3·0
1·015	2·2	3·0	4·1
1·020	2·8	4·0	5·3
1·025	3·5	5·0	6·5
1·030	4·2	6·0	7·7
1·035	4·7	7·0	8·8
1·040	5·6	8·0	9·9
1·045	6·2	9·0	11·1
1·050	6·9	10·0	12·3
1·055	7·5	11·0	13·4
1·060	8·2	12·0	14·5
1·065	8·8	13·0	15·7
1·070	9·5	14·0	16·9
1·075	10·0	15·0	18·0
1·080	10·7	16·0	19·2
1·085	11·4	17·0	20·4
1·090	12·0	18·9	21·5
1·095	12·4	19·0	22·6
1·100	13·2	20·0	23·7

Undoubtedly the hydrometer to choose is one employing the ordinary specific gravity scale. You can obtain hydrometers with the following ranges:

$$
\begin{array}{ccc}
0·900 & \text{to} & 1·000 \\
1·000 & \text{to} & 1·100 \\
1·100 & \text{to} & 1·200 \\
0·990 & \text{to} & 1·170 \\
\end{array}
$$

The last-mentioned range will cover everything you require and there is one excellent hydrometer on the market which shows at a glance the S.G., the sugar content and the potential alcoholic content. If you are doing experimental work or require for convenience a scale with larger and more readable gradations, you can buy the set of three. If you cannot get them all at once, plump for the one which gives the middle range, 1·000 to 1·100, adding the others when you can.

To find the specific gravity of a liquid, place the hydrometer in the trial jar and pour in the liquid until the hydrometer floats free. Push it down once or twice with your finger tip, and spin it to free it of any bubbles, which will affect the reading. The reading should be taken with the eye at surface level, and do not be misled by the false reading caused by the meniscus. The true reading is where the main surface level of the liquid would cut the scale, and *not* where the meniscus, caused by surface tension, does. That false reading will be a slightly lower specific gravity.

Obviously the scale records all the degrees of comparative

heaviness, hence its great use to us. There is one special point to remember: specific gravity is affected by temperature. Accordingly the hydrometer scale is graduated at a prescribed temperature. The figure is always shown on the scale and is usually about 60°F. (16°C.). If the temperature of the liquid you are testing is 10F.° (6C.°) or more above or below that stated on the hydrometer, then an allowance must be made and an adjusted reading must be calculated.

The following table shows the variations clearly and simply:

| Temperature in Degrees | | Correction to the Last Figure |
Centigrade	Fahrenheit	of the Specific Gravity Reading
10	50	Subtract 0·6
15	59	No correction necessary
20	68	Add 0·9
25	77	Add 2·0
30	86	Add 3·4
35	95	Add 5·0
40	104	Add 6·8

For example a sample of must at a temperature of 95°F. (35°C.) is found to have a specific gravity of 1·115. We see from the table that at 95°F. a correction of 5 has to be added to the last figure of the specific gravity reading. Therefore: 1·115 + 5 = 1·120, which is the true specific gravity of the must in question.

The hydrometer, it should be explained, will only give you a reading showing the sugar content of a liquid (really "saccharometer" would be a better description of it, for our purposes). The remainder of the information you require is obtained by using that reading in conjunction with tables, or, if you prefer, graphs. For simplicity's sake we have adhered to the tabular system.

The hydrometer, you will find, will give you surprisingly accurate results; when it is used, for instance, for determining the strength of a wine the winemaker using a hydrometer will arrive at a result very close indeed to that which would obtained by laboratory distillation or by use of an expensive ebullioscope. By no means the same can be said of the vinometer, another method.

Despite this general accuracy, one occasionally comes across exceptions, and it should be emphasized that the tables we give are liable to small inaccuracies at either end of the scale. At the start of the ferment there is some clouding by suspended solids and from bubbles, and towards the end of the ferment alcohol is present in increasing quantities. Alcohol is less dense than water and prevents an entirely accurate measurement of the amount of sugar still in the wine. That is what we are principally concerned with—the amount of sugar in the must and the amount of alcohol likely to be produced from it during fermentation.

Sometimes this clouding can occur, but usually the hydrometer is accurate, and the preceding table will be found to be a most useful general guide. The "potential alcoholic content" is the amount of alcohol which would be produced if the sugar were "fermented right out", i.e. if all the sugar in the wine were used up, in which case the specific gravity will usually be below 1·000, because of the presence of alcohol.

Specific Gravity	Potential % alcohol by volume	Amount of sugar in the Imp. gallon		Amount of sugar in the U.S. gallon		Amount of sugar added to Imp. gal.		Amount of sugar added to U.S. gal.		Volume with sugar added of 1 Imp. gal.		Volume with sugar added of 1 U.S. gal.	
		lb.	oz.	lb.	oz.	lb.	oz.	lb.	oz.	gal.	fl. oz.	gal.	fl. oz.
1·010	0·9		2		1·7		2·5		2·1	1	1	1	0·8
1·015	1·6		4		3·4		5		4·2	1	3	1	2·4
1·020	2·3		7		5·8		8		6·7	1	5	1	4
1·025	3·0		9		7·5		10		8·3	1	7	1	5·6
1·030	3·7		12		10		13		10·8	1	8	1	6·4
1·035	4·4		15		12·5	1	0		13·3	1	10	1	8
1·040	5·1	1	1		14	1	2		15	1	11	1	8·8
1·045	5·8	1	3		15·8	1	4	1	0·7	1	13	1	10·4
1·050	6·5	1	5	1	1·5	1	7	1	3·3	1	14	1	11·2
1·055	7·2	1	7	1	3	1	9	1	4·8	1	16	1	12·8
1·060	7·8	1	9	1	5	1	11	1	6·5	1	17	1	13·6
1·065	8·6	1	11	1	6·5	1	14	1	9	1	19	1	15·2
1·070	9·2	1	13	1	8	2	1	1	11·5	1	20	1	16
1·075	9·9	1	15	1	9·8	2	4	1	14	1	22	1	17·6
1·080	10·6	2	1	1	11·5	2	6	1	15·6	1	23	1	18·4
1·085	11·3	2	4	1	14	2	9	2	2·2	1	25	1	20
1·090	12·0	2	6	1	15·6	2	12	2	4·6	1	27	1	21·6
1·095	12·7	2	8	2	1·3	2	15	2	7·2	1	28	1	22·4
1·100	13·4	2	10	2	3	3	2	2	9·6	1	30	1	24
1·105	14·1	2	12	2	4·6	3	5	2	12·1	1	32	1	25·6
1·110	14·9	2	14	2	6·3	3	8	2	14·6	1	33	1	26·4
1·115	15·6	3	0	2	8	3	11	3	1·1	1	35	1	28
1·120	16·3	3	2	2	9·6	3	14	3	3·6	1	37	1	29·6
1·125	17·0	3	4	2	11·3	4	1	3	6·1	1	38	1	30·4
1·130	17·7	3	6	2	12·9	4	4	3	8·6	1	40	1	32
1·135	18·4	3	8	2	14·6	4	7	3	11·1	1	42	1	33·6

By using this table one can decide how much sugar to use in making any particular wine, and by using the hydrometer regularly one can keep a close check on the progress of the ferment, i.e. the speed with which the sugar is being converted by the yeast.

Now let us look at the use of the hydrometer in detail, and the various purposes for which it can be utilized:

To find how much natural sugar is present:

Test the juice or liquid as already described. If you are making wine from an undiluted fruit juice, the specific gravity may be quite high, 1·035 or 1·040, but with the average country wine, where the juice is normally heavily diluted with water, it will be much lower, and often so low that the natural sugar content can be virtually ignored. By referring to the table you can see exactly how much natural sugar is present, e.g. with a specific gravity of 1·035 you would know that in every Imperial gallon of the must there is 15 ozs. of natural sugar.

To find the amount of sugar present in terms of a percentage, take the last three figures of the specific gravity, multiply by 2·15, and divide the result by 10. Thus:

$$\text{Specific gravity 1·035. Sugar content} = \frac{35 \times 2\cdot15}{10} = 7\cdot52\%$$

To find the potential alcohol content of the must:

Once you have obtained the specific gravity, refer to the table, and you can see at a glance what percentage of alcohol by volume will be produced if all the sugar is worked out. (Our figures, it should be noted, are deliberately on the conservative side.)

To calculate sugar addition, using the Imperial table:

Knowing how much sugar you already have, it is easy to decide how much to add to produce a wine of the strength you desire. (Below 10% alcohol, a wine may not keep.) In the example quoted, for instance, a wine made from the natural juice would be under 5%. Perhaps you would like to make one containing 13½% alcohol by volume.

By referring to the table we see that this would require an initial specific gravity of 1·100, or 2 lbs. 10 ozs. sugar per gallon of must. Since we already have 15 ozs., we shall require to add 1 lb. 11 ozs. in all. Incidentally, it may be noted that 2¼ oz. of sugar added to 1 Imperial gal. of must will raise the gravity by approximately 5 degrees.)

Diluting:

If the gravity of syrup or must is too high to be measured with a hydrometer, or if you require to reduce the acidity of a juice, it may be necessary to dilute it. If you add one equal quantity of water the *gravity* (not the specific gravity) will be reduced by a half, e.g. from 180 to 90 (or from 1·180 to 1·090). The acidity will likewise be 'reduced by half. Dilution can be calculated accordingly.

Keeping a check on the progress of the ferment.

As the ferment proceeds, so the specific gravity of the liquid will drop, rapidly at first, and then more slowly, and it is by the *speed* of the drop that one can judge how much sugar to add to keep the ferment going yet still produce a dry wine. As we have said elsewhere, the biggest difficulty for the average winemaker is that of producing a strong, *dry* wine, and the simplest way to achieve this is to use a hydrometer at the outset, to determine how much total sugar will be needed to produce the strength of wine desired. Add, at the outset, half the quantity, but keep a careful check every 2 or 3 days with the hydrometer to see how things are going. The first drop will be considerable, probably 40 degrees or so in a few days, but after that the *rate* of drop will diminish, until finally it may be taking 2 or 3 weeks to effect a drop of 2 or 3 degrees. This is when the wine is nearly finished, and it is then dangerous to add too much sugar, if an oversweet wine is to be avoided.

Consequently, it is a good plan, as we say, to add half the total sugar at the outset, and the remainder in 4-oz. lots *according to the speed of drop,* each time the specific gravity approaches 1·000.

If, when you are making a dry wine (i.e. have not added sugar for sweetening), the gravity ceases to drop when it is still comparatively high (say 40-60), it indicates plainly that the fermentation has "stuck", or temporarily ceased, and must be restarted if possible, as described elsewhere.

If your final specific gravity drops below 1·000, congratulate yourself, for the chances are that you have produced a really strong, dry wine, since there is sufficient alcohol present to "dilute" the water below its normal gravity.

Calculating the strength of the finished wine:

Finally, and perhaps most interesting of all, you can tell with some degree of accuracy the strength of your finished wine. This, however, can only be done if you record the specific gravity of the must *after* the sugar is added, but before fermentation has begun. At the end of the fermentation, take the specific gravity reading again. The final reading is subtracted from the first, giving the "drop" caused by the ferment, and this is divided by 7·36, giving the percentage of alcohol by volume in the finished wine.

E.g.   Initial specific gravity = 1.100
        Final specific gravity = 1·000
                        Drop = 100

$$\frac{100}{7\cdot36} = 13\cdot5\% \text{ alcohol by volume.}$$

A point to note here is that the same system can be used even if you are adding sugar by stages, *as long as you keep a record of the drop in degrees between successive additions of sugar.* Add up all the drops, and the total is the figure to be divided by 7·36 as before. This is an approximate result but will in normal cases be accurate enough for the average winemaker.

For quick reference use the following table:

Drop in Specific Gravity	Percentage of Alcohol by Volume
10	1·4
20	2·7
30	4·1
40	5·4
50	6·8
60	8·2
70	9·5
80	10·9
90	12·2
100	13·6
110	15·0
120	16·3
130	17·7
140	19·0

To turn the strength in percentage of alcohol into terms of U.S. proof spirit, multiply by 2, thus:

13·5% alcohol by volume = 13·5 × 2 = 27 U.S. Proof.

For Canadian Proof values under Proof strength of 57·1%, multiply by $\frac{7}{4}$ and subtract the result from 100, thus:

13·5% alcohol by volume = $100 - \frac{13\cdot5 \times 7}{4}$ = 100 - 23.6

= 76·4 Under Proof·

A table of comparison of various proofs will be found on page 119.

The final specific gravity gives valuable guidance in the classification and therefore the use of the wine. If it is dry (1·000 or below and strong it will be excellent as an aperitif, like a dry sherry; if it is dry, and not too strong (10-12%) it will be excellent as a table wine. If it is strong and medium sweet (1·001-1·014) or strong and sweet (1·015 and above) it is best kept for dessert purposes or for making into liqueurs. The general principle is that the later in a meal the wine is served, the stronger it should be.

Another good rule of thumb is: the stronger the wine, the longer it should be allowed to mature. Weak wines are usually drunk young.

From this chapter we hope it will be seen that the regular use of the hydrometer really has much to recommend it, for it can remove most of the guesswork from winemaking and add a great deal to the interest of the craft.

Chapter 10
ALCOHOL & CO.

T HE DIFFERENCE between fruit cordials, beers, wines and spirits depends to a large extent on the widely different quantities of alcohol present in the liquor. Fruit cordial, of course, has none and so can be drunk in quantity without any intoxicating effect. Beer has an alcoholic content of about 5% by volume. Unfortified wine varies between 8% and 18%. The weaker wines do not keep very well and, like beer, have to be drunk relatively soon. Spirits contain about 40% alcohol by volume and such a high concentration of alcohol enables the spirit to be kept for up to 100 years. The stronger wines will keep for many years too, but whether our wines go on improving after 3 years or so is doubtful. This reference is of course to fruit and flower wines, etc., and not to grape wines. Claret takes many years to mature and so, too, does port.

It is the alcohol which gives wine that different satisfaction from a non-alcoholic drink. It has an agreeable "wine-like" odour and a warming and stimulating effect, quickly entering the blood stream and so to the head and the knees! It is alcohol which in combination with acids and their derivatives gives wine its bouquet and flavour.

The alcohol in wine consists almost entirely of ethyl alcohol but sometimes there are minute quantities of the other alcohols present such as amyl, butyl and propyl which together make up fusel oil. In fruit or flower wines there is rarely any trace of fusel oil but in wines prepared from grains, cereals or potatoes it is quite likely that some of the higher alcohols will be present. Fusel oil, as everyone knows, is highly poisonous if any measurable quantity is consumed. In a bottle of wine there is little likelihood of there being more than a trace or so, but in alcohol which has not been distilled by an expert chemist it is possible that the quantity of fusel oil could be increased by concentration to a degree dangerous to health. Hence the advice, do not distil your own spirits.

Also present in the wine are a number of acids, some of which combine with alcohol to form esters. Notably there are citric acid and tartaric acid and we have already seen that these two acids are needed for a variety of reasons. Then there is succinic acid which gives that distinctive "winy flavour", and also lactic acid and malic acid. The latter, two, in the proportion of about 5 parts malic acid to 1 of lactic, control the sharp taste of the acid.

The tartaric acid, though soluble in water, is insoluble in

alcohol and as the quantity of alcohol increases the tartaric acid precipitates as cream of tartar; the colder the wine the heavier the precipitation—hence the need to store maturing wine in a cool place.

A microbe of the *bacterium gracile* family sometimes starts a slight bottle fermentation known as a malo-lactic ferment and converts much of the malic acid, with its pronounced sharpness, to lactic acid, which has a less noticeable flavour. It is this kind of action in a much more complicated form which causes a wine to mellow as it matures. Although biologically speaking there is no "life" in wine, we speak of it as a living thing, because of the chemical changes which slowly continue during the whole life of a bottle of wine.

The small amount of oxygen dissolved in wine when it is bottled, added to that in the air between the wine and the cork, oxidizes a tiny quantity of alcohol and forms acetaldehyde which gives a lovely aroma to wine. Acetaldehyde in turn combines with a minute quantity of alcohol and forms acetal which provides yet another ester. You can now see the value of leaving a space about an inch under the cork to help in the formation of these lovely odours. *But* do be careful not to overdo the oxygenation in case this delicate chemical process gets out of hand and goes too far, oxidizing too much of the alcohol and forming acetic acid and carbon dioxide. With sufficient alcohol the wine could "break up", becoming flat and lifeless. Furthermore a reasonable degree of alcohol keeps many of the bacteria in check. For example mycoderma aceti are overcome by an alcoholic strength of more than 10% by volume, so if your wine is strong enough and kept sealed it will not turn to vinegar, nor will it decompose.

It will be clear that alcohol in wine serves many purposes. Firstly it gives the wine that satisfying taste, secondly by combination with different acids and aldehydes it gives wine a lovely bouquet. Thirdly, in sufficient quantities it preserves wine from deterioration by bacterial infection.

As well as the acids and alcohols wine also contains glycerine, really another alcohol, which is formed during the chemically highly complex process of fermentation. As much as 3% may be present and this gives the wine a smoothness to the palate and a richness that can be seen when you swirl the wine in a glass and watch it descend slowly. The glycerine adds body to the wine and tends to adhere to the glass during swirling, and returns more slowly to the level than the alcohol and other contents. The glycerine also helps to mask acidity.

Finally, there are also a number of volatile esters of other acids present, notably of propionic acid and valerianic acid. These esters slowly disappear into the bouquet of a wine when a bottle is opened.

Chapter 11

HYGIENE AND THE USES OF SULPHITE

ANYONE PREPARING food or drink of any sort should naturally set about it hygienically, or the "end product" may be not only unpleasant but positively harmful. In winemaking the strictest cleanliness is even more necessary because one is dealing with a fermentation process and the making of a wine, from start to finish, may be spread over several months. This being so, there is far more opportunity for bacterial infection than in, say, cookery, and it pays to take commonsense precautions.

Much of the equipment we use affords hiding places for bacteria if not kept scrupulously clean—a crack in a wooden spoon or paddle, used for stirring one batch of must and put away damp, the cracks between the staves of a barrel, a porous and unsterilized used cork, a bottle or jar containing the lees of an old ferment, a leaky tap to a cask, damaged fruit, unsterilized bottles—all these are potent sources of infection.

The biggest single enemy we have to combat, of course, is the vinegar bacterium, which can be airborne but which is most likely to be introduced into your wine by that obnoxious carrier, the vinegar fly. Vinegar flies are the tiny flies one sees around compost heaps or rotten fruit. They appear as if by magic if you leave a ferment exposed, and it is always essential, therefore, to cover closely with a plastic sheet, a thick cloth, or several layers of thin cloth, a ferment which may be in an open crock. And always use a fermentation lock during the secondary fermentation.

Vinegar flies, it should be noted, are very persistent and will find their way through comparatively small cracks, or through small holes in a cloth. They will, too, even crawl inside the spout of a wine tap or a wine-damp piece of small-bore glass tubing. And one fly can well infect a whole brew . . . so it pays to take precautions.

The first rule of hygiene therefore is:

Always protect your brew from the vinegar fly.

Even doing this, however, is of little avail if the ingredients of your must were infected even before you introduced your chosen yeast and set the fermentation in train. Fruit in its natural state, for example, is host to many unwanted airborne yeasts and bacteria. which it is as well to eliminate at the outset, and the same is true of dried fruit, grain, and other ingredients we commonly use.

71

The simplest form of sterilization, where it is possible, is to pour boiling water over the ingredients (as distinct from boiling them *in* the water, which may lead to pectin-clouded wines), but with some delicate-flavoured wines this is not to be recommended and we have to cast about for an alternative method which will enable us to use cold water.

It is here that sulphur dioxide can be so useful, and in advocating its use we are really proposing nothing revolutionary, for sulphiting is invariably practised at one stage or another by most European vignerons, who would not dream of adding a good wine yeast to an impure must. By employing this chemical, too, the winemaker can remove much of the drudgery from his hobby, and avoid tiresome, repeated bottle-washing, and sterilization by more clumsy methods, such as "baking in the oven", which are sometimes recommended—baking, we know, has led to many broken 1-gal. glass jars.

Sulphur dioxide, in short, can be used for sterilizing barrels, your press, fermentation jars, corks, equipment and bottles: it will improve your wine, prevent diseases and oxidation (i.e. browning), stabilize a wine, keep stored barrels, jars or bottles sweet, and sterilize unfermented fruit juices for storage. Anything which has all these manifold advantages is obviously something which the winemaker cannot afford to be without, particularly since it is cheap and easy to obtain.

Ever since mediaeval days sulphite has been used for barrel sterilization, but this was done by burning in the barrel sulphur matches (which are still obtainable) or sulphur in a ladle. The gas given off is the required sulphur dioxide (SO_2), which has a pungent smell rather like that of smelling salts, but the snag of this method is that it is difficult to estimate exactly how much sulphite is released or enters the wine.

Nowadays things are simpler, for we can obtain our sulphite from a solid salt of sulphurous acid, i.e. sodium metabisulphite or potassium metabisulphite (the two are interchangeable for winemaking purposes). The simplest way to obtain the chemical used to be to buy a bottle of Campden tablets (ordinary fruit preserving tablets) but nowadays, owing to changed methods of preserving fruit, they are not always easy to come by in drugstores although most winemaking supplies firms carry them.

If you can obtain some—they are quite cheap—keep them in a screw-capped, air tight bottle until used.

Each tablet contains 7 grains (or 0·45 gram) of bisulphite, and one in a gallon of water will give a solution of 50 parts per million of sulphur dioxide.

An eighth of a tablet can be used in the U-bend of the fermentation trap, and will render the trap bacteria-proof, whereas it will not be so if you use plain water. With water, a vinegar fly may meet a miserable death by drowning, but the bacteria it carries will infect the water in the trap, the "inner" end of which is in aerial contact with the wine, so that it may turn to vinegar even though a trap has been used. Note, too, that the sulphite solution will need to be changed every month or so, since it will deteriorate. Alternatively, plug the top of the fermentation trap with a tiny tuft of cotton wool to deny flies access, or use in the U-bend glycerine of borax.

Purifying the must. Winemakers are not always clear as to the purpose of adding sulphite to the must before fermentation. The object is to suppress unwanted yeasts or bacteria which may be present naturally in order to allow the chosen wine yeast to do its work. "But surely," you may ask, "if I suppress wild yeasts I also suppress the wine yeast?" The answer is that we use only sufficient sulphite to suppress the wild yeasts, and that 24 hrs. later its action has abated sufficiently for the vigorous wine yeast, introduced in a much greater quantity, to overcome it.

We are *not*, it should be noted, *sterilizing* the must, strictly speaking, i.e. we are not making it impossible to ferment; to do that we would need ten times the quantity of sulphite we use. What we *are* doing is to *purify* it considerably, and for that purpose two Campden tablets per gallon will be found sufficient, and often are. If your fruit seems sound and you have no reason to suspect it, use one tablet per gallon of must, but if you are at all doubtful, use two.

The second rule of hygiene therefore is:

> *If you have not used boiling water, add one or two Campden tablets to your must 24 hrs. before introducing your chosen yeast.*

Preventing oxidation. Sometimes a finished wine, light in colour, turns brown after having been exposed to the air for 24 hrs. or so. This is known as oxidation (many brown sherries are oxidized wines) and it can be prevented (not cured) by adding one Campden tablet per gallon to the bulk of wine.

Terminating fermentation. Very occasionnally, too, it will be desired to *stop* a wine fermenting when it has reached a desired strength and sweetness, and this can usually be done by adding one or two Campden tablets per gallon. Combined with the alcohol which has been produced, this is usually sufficient to stabilize any wine. It may be necessary to uncork a wine sulphited in this way two or three hours before drinking, in case there is a slight odour (one often has to do this with commercial wines); the taste will be unaffected.

Campden tablets are useful, of course, in treating several "ailments" of wine, because of their anti-bacterial qualities, but this is fully dealt with in Chapter 20.

Sterilizing containers and equipment. It is here that sulphite is most useful of all. Crush six Campden tablets, dissolve them in a pint of water, and add ½ oz. citric acid, and you have the most valuable all-purpose sterilizing solution. It pays to make up a quantity in a Winchester (½ gal.) and keep it well closed with a rubber stopper so that it is always handy when required.

A little of it can be made to sterilize a large number of bottles by pouring it from one to the other through a funnel, each being in turn corked and thoroughly agitated, so that the solution reaches every part of the interior. (Any sediment or old yeast adhering to the bottle should first be removed with water and a bottle brush.) Make sure, too, that you wipe round the neck of the bottle thoroughly with a cloth dipped in the solution.

Barrels can be cleaned in the same way, and your press and other equipment can be made safe by being wiped with, or immersed in, the solution. Taps of barrels in the "cellar" should also be wiped over occasionally.

A sulphite solution is also most useful when jars and bottles have to be stored. When they have been sterilized as above, put an inch or so of sulphite solution in the bottom of them, cork them, and put them away. When they are required for use all that is then necessary is to pour away the sulphite (or use it for another purpose) and wash the outside of the bottle. If the bottle is to be used for fermenting, it is as well to give it a quick internal rinse with water as well, but if it is to be used for a finished wine this is not necessary.

A third rule therefore is:

Keep all containers and equipment clean and sterilized.

As already mentioned you may find it difficult nowadays to buy Campden tablets. In that case, do not despair, but make up your solution direct with chemical itself.

Buy from your winemaking supplier 1 lb. of potassium metabisulphite ($K_2S_2O_5$ ... if he asks!), crush the crystals in some warm water, and make the quantity up to 1 Imperial gallon (or use ½ kilo of crystals in 5 litres of water). This will be your stock solution, to be diluted for various purposes as necessary. Actually it is a 10% solution, but in practice may be considered as containing 5% by weight of the active gas.

Your stock solution can be used for just the same purposes as the Campden tablets, as follows:

To purify the must prior to fermentation: 3½ fluid ozs. of the solution to each 10 gals. (or ⅓ fl. oz. per gallon, or 10 ml. per 5 litres).

To sterilize the must completely (or to sterilize a non-fermented fruit juice for safe storage) you will have to add 32 fl. ozs. to every 10 Imperial gals., or 1 part of solution to 50 parts of must; up to double that quantity may be necessary in hot weather.

To sterilize corks, barrel, bottles, apparatus: 1 pt. of the stock solution to 9 pts. of water. This can also be used for keeping stored bottles, jars etc. sweet, as above.

Boiling. Although it is wiser to avoid the actual boiling of ingredients where possible, boiling water offers a simple form of sterilization, and is particularly valuable for dealing with apparatus which will not be harmed by it. Siphons, rubber tubing, wooden spoons and paddles, crushers, sieves, test-tubes, bungs, spile-pegs, wine-casks and their taps, and glass fermentation traps, for instance, are all conveniently sterilized by immersion in, or use of, boiling water, if one has no sulphite solution handy.

In the cellar. We have dealt principally with hygiene in the making of wine, but also one needs to observe commonsense precautions in the "wine cellar", however small or large it may be. Some of us are lucky enough to be able to have a separate shed or room set aside for the purpose, others may have to make do with "the cupboard under the stairs", the larder, or an odd corner or cupboard, but wherever wine is made or kept commonsense precautions should be observed. "Commonsense" in that little is required beyond cleanliness and the frequent use of sulphite as suggested.

The room or cellar itself should be clean and free of accumulations of old corks and containers holding dregs of previous brews, both of which are potent sources of infection. Old corks should be kept separate from new. Bottles, as they are emptied, should be cleaned, have a little sulphite put in them, and then be corked and put neatly away.

Whenever you are winemaking, tidy up as soon as you have finished, and always be careful to mop up with a sulphited mop or cloth any little pools or circles of wine which may result from racking or bottling operations, and likewise be careful to mop up any frothy overflow from a ferment conducted in a barrel.

Incidentally, it is not a good plan to insert a tap in the cask from the outset, for it then has to remain there for perhaps a year before the wine is consumed. If this is the case, there will be a tendency for the tap to grow mould, and, even worse, a tendency for it to leak after it has been used the first time. This is a great nuisance, for not only can one lose a lot of wine in a short space of time, if the leak is serious, but one is bothered with pools of wine on the floor, which invite disaster. A dripping tap can be a real nuisance.

It is better, therefore, to hammer home a cork in the taphole and cut it off flush with the wood. When the time comes it is quite easy to tap the barrel.

Last rule, then:

Be a methodical and cleanly cellarman!

To sum up, keep your store-room or cellar as clean as possible, and allow no untidiness or liquid rubbish to lie about which may be an open invitation to the vinegar fly. Keep your ferments always covered, or under an air-lock, use sulphite freely, and sterilize your equipment regularly—and all will be well!

Chapter 12

PREPARING THE MUST

SOME UNCOUTH philistine once remarked that you can make wine from old boots! While we do not know anyone who has ever attempted to do so, we have met people who have made "wine" from water, sugar, nutrient and yeast!

Fortunately there is a bountiful variety of excellent ingredients that can be used to make delightful wines. Many flowers can be used and an even greater number of fruits. And for those not always able to take opportunity of fresh fruits and blossoming flowers there are many dried fruits and dried flowers that can be made into wine at will. Grains, roots and vegetables are almost humdrum in their suitability, and tea wine is delicious. Concentrated grape juice can also now be bought in small quantities to produce excellent red and white wines, at little more than a quarter a bottle.

It is not proposed to discuss here the preparation of the must of every wine. Further details will be given with the recipes. Sufficient at this stage to discuss the general principles which should be applied to the appropriate recipes.

To extract the necessary juice and flavour certain recipes suggest that the basic ingredient such as parsnips or beetroot should be boiled. If boiling is necessary great care should be taken to avoid overcooking either by too vigorous or too prolonged a boiling—an obstinately cloudy wine might ensue. Usually it is sufficient to bring the ingredients to the boil rapidly and then simmer gently till the root or fruit is just tender. In this way a high extraction rate is obtained without too much loss of flavour in the steam. It is not necessary to boil your ingredients in the full quantity of water to be used. There is no reason why you should not use only as much water as your container will conveniently hold during the boiling and add the remaining water when you strain off the pulp. The additional water may be cold or hot. It doesn't matter. But avoid boiling if possible.

For most recipes it is sufficient to pour boiling water over the ingredients, stirring thoroughly, macerating the fruit if need be and steeping for 2 or 3 days in a closely covered vessel. Some winemakers are of the opinion that boiling water is too drastic in its action and that its advantages of sterilizing the fruit and the more quickly extracting the flavour are outweighed by disadvantages—especially the dissipation of delicate volatile flavours and essences. If boiling water is not used then sulphite in one form or another should certainly be added to safeguard the must from infection. We favour the use of boiling water for most recipes while recognizing that exceptions should occasionally be made.

With certain fruits—notably red grapes, plums and the like—it is necessary to ferment on the pulp. By this means a high colour extraction is obtained. With red grapes, fermentation begins soon after pressing to release the juice. Over the next few days the colour which is in the skin is leached into the must. When a must is being fermented in the presence of the pulp it is necessary to break up and press down the "cap" several times a day. The bubbles of carbon dioxide get under the pulp and lift up the tightly packed mass into the air above. This not only removes the pulp from the liquid, so that the extraction cannot continue, but also provides a first-class objective for acetobacter, the vinegar bacillus, otherwise known as mycoderma aceti. This cap, or crust, must be broken up with a wooden spoon and pushed below the surface of the fermenting liquid several times a day. The ferment should be encouraged to be as vigorous as possible and a thick cloth should be kept over the necessarily wide crock.

Wines made from dried flowers are often very popular, especially with the city dweller who has no access to coltsfoot, agrimony and the like. Packets of dried flowers can be bought for about 50¢ from most herbalists and are simple to use. Experience teaches, however, that they are best used as flavourings for wines that are somewhat lacking in this essential ingredient. Wines made from potatoes, or from grains like wheat or rice, benefit considerably from an infusion of, for example, dried coltsfoot or marigold flowers. Two ounces of dried flowers are sufficient for 1 Imperial gal. of wine. Just soak the flowers in a small quantity of boiling water, stirring and macerating with a wooden spoon on and off for 2 or 3 hrs., strain off the water and repeat the process to make sure that all the essence has been extracted. Add the liquid to the must prior to fermentation.

Leaves, such as from a walnut tree, also give a pleasant flavour to a wine. You can buy them dry, but can use 30 or 40 fresh leaves instead. They can be infused separately or soaked with the other ingredients since they will be strained off before fermentation.

Herbs are used similarly and a wonderful variety are available. Two ounces are sufficient for the gallon together with 1 lb. wheat or barley or rice and 1 lb. of raisins and the juice and rind of two large lemons together with sugar, nutrient and yeast of course.

An unusual basic ingredient, and alas! one not readily available to many people, is birch sap. The tree must be tapped during the first two weeks in March when the sap is rising, but any fully grown silver birch tree will do. Maple sap can be substituted, where available. A detailed recipe is given on page 203.

Under the skin of fruit there are a number of enzymes, one of which is known as pectinase. When the fruit is mashed in water and left in a warm atmosphere pectinase dissolves the pectin walls of the cells containing juice. If the fruit is boiled the enzymes are destroyed and it may be necessary to add commercially produced enzyme to break down the pectin. If this is not done, the pectin may later form a gelatinous solution. In jam-making pectin is needed to help the jam to jell and set, in winemaking we want to remove the pectin so that the wine will clear and be free from haze.

It is possible to add extra pectinase in the form of Pectolase. This also helps to extract the fullest goodness from the pulp. As little as ¼ oz. of Pectolase is sufficient for 8 lbs. of fruit pulp, (2 grams per Kilo.), but the temperature should be around blood heat for the best results, Pectolase can safely be added to every fruit must. It is more difficult for pectinase to work in the presence of much sugar, and accordingly Pectolase should be added before the sugar, and left for a day or so to fulfil its purpose.

To sum up then, fruit pectin is dissolved by pectinase which is also present in all fruit. There may not be sufficient pectinase, however, to dissolve all the pectin and the pectinase may itself be destroyed by heat. It can, therefore, be added to fruit mashes in the form of Pectolase, to dissolve the pectin and secure better juice extraction. Leave for a day or two in a warm place before straining and adding sugar.

When the pulp is ready for straining it is important to use a substantial cloth. Muslin is not really strong enough as the weave is so open. A nylon sieve is much superior, but if this is not available a good linen cloth will do. It is sometimes helpful to use a colander first to remove large pulp masses, straining only the smaller pieces with the linen.

Careful straining at this stage removes the tiny particles of pulp which otherwise remain suspended in solution and cause a cloudy wine. This pulp is of no further importance to the wine. Sometimes it settles as a sludge, but obviously it is better if it can be excluded. A nylon sieve pays for itself over and over again in this connection.

Having extracted the juice, the next stage is the check on acidity. The simplest way is by testing the must. Many people are able to look at a length or height and say "that is so many

feet" or "so many inches" and when it is measured these figures
are found to be surprisingly accurate. A decorator can look at
a room and say from experience that so many rolls of paper will
be required. So it is with the winemaker, who has tasted a
number of musts and made several gallons of wine. He can
quickly say, from his theoretical knowledge and practical experience, that a little more acid is necessary or not as the case may
be. Those who feel the need to make some sort of check should
consult the chapter on "Acidity".

If it is necessary to increase the acidity, citric acid is added as
required, either in the form of crystals or lemon juice. If fresh
lemon juice is used, it should be strained before mixing into the
wine. This keeps out unwanted portions of lemon pulp. All
roots, grains, flowers, vegetables and dried fruits require acid.

It will be appreciated that in the dilution of the acid with
water, other substances will be diluted too. Except for red grapes,
pears and crab-apples, all the diluted juices of all fruits, roots,
flowers and grains need additional tannin. This may be added
as a ¼ teaspoonful of grape tannin or a tablespoonful of cold
strong tea that has steeped overlong.

So far, then, the juice has been extracted, by careful boiling
or by steeping in hot water for 2 or 3 days or in cold water for
7 to 10 days. If fruit is the main ingredient Pectolase has been
added. Acidity has been corrected and tannin added if necessary. The next stage in preparing the must for fermentation is the
addition of sugar. The quantity to be added can be decided by
a simple rule of thumb or more accurately by a hydrometer. As
a whole chapter has been devoted to this valuable instrument we
will confine ourselves here to the rule of thumb. In discussing
the quantity and kind of sugar to be added consideration should
first be given to the kind of wine you are proposing to make. A
dry light table wine will obviously need less sugar than a strong
sweet dessert wine. The kind of sugar is almost immaterial.
Brown sugar will colour and alter the flavour of white wines and
so is best reserved for strongly flavoured red wines. Granulated
white sugar is most convenient to use for white wines, especially
if you can obtain cane sugar. Invert sugar is excellent if you can
afford it.

As far as quantity is concerned it should be remembered that
when no natural sugar is present 2½ lbs. of sugar dissolved in
an Imperial gallon of must should ferment to dryness and give
an alcoholic content of about 12½%. For table purposes this
is entirely adequate, being quite strong enough to keep well and
not too strong to drink with a meal. For a medium sweet wine
that may ferment to about 16% you should use not more than

3 lbs. of sugar. If you want a wine a little stronger and sweeter then up to another 8 ozs. of sugar may be added in 4-oz. portions during fermentation.

The initial sugar may be added in dry form to the must, but should be thoroughly dissolved by stirring before being left. Sugar added during fermentation should first be dissolved in some of the wine taken out for the purpose. The sweetened wine should be returned very slowly to the bulk of the wine, otherwise foaming will occur and wine may be lost.

It is not always possible to get a yeast to ferment beyond an alcoholic content of about 14% and if you have added sugar sufficient for a higher alcoholic conversion and failed to attain it, then your wine will be oversweet and far below your expectations. We cannot recommend too strongly that it is far preferable to achieve dryness with say 2½ lbs. sugar and then to add a few ounces more sugar. If fermentation begins again, so much the better, if it doesn't then your wine will have no more than the dry edge taken off. It will certainly be much more palatable than a too sweet wine.

Only one other ingredient is now needed beside the yeast, and that is the yeast nutrient. Full details have already been given of the contents of yeast nutrient and you can either make up your own or use a ready prepared tablet. The latter are very hard and need crushing before adding to the must. Except when using fresh grape juice or grape juice concentrate, yeast nutrient is absolutely essential to secure a good fermentation to a high degree of alcohol.

The must is at last ready for fermentation. It should be given a thorough stir to aid oxygenation and then be poured into a jar or barrel. For the first few days the ferment may be tumultuous and it is as well to have the barrel or jar no more than seven-eighths full so that any foaming does not enter the fermentation trap. Before fitting the trap, however, an actively fermenting yeast should be added. A pure culture wine yeast is best, prepared as already indicated. As soon as the yeast is in the must, screw the fermentation trap into a bored cork or rubber stopper and press this into the neck of the jar.

Finally drop one-eighth of a Campden tablet into the open end of the trap and pour in a few drops of boiled water. This will permit the carbon dioxide to bubble through, but prevent infection of any kind from entering. Fermentation will start almost at once.

Chapter 13
FERMENTATION IN PRACTICE

IN THE last chapter the must was prepared ready for fermentation. Now about the actual process. It is always best to use a pure wine yeast, either a general purpose sedimentary yeast of the saccharomyces ellipsoideus variety or a particular strain of that variety. You can use a culture on agar in a test-tube, liquid yeast or dried pressed yeast tablets, but whatever kind you use, it is important to prepare the yeast at least 48 hrs. before adding it to the must. By doing this you can be sure that the yeast is actively reproducing itself before you use it. One cannot be certain that all the yeast cells in a preparation are alive and in fact many of them are exhausted and dead. By preparing the yeast as described on page 42, the other cells are able to rehabilitate themselves and to multiply in a perfect setting, so making a sufficient quantity of vigorously living cells to start their work of fermentation.

To give the yeast the best possible chance it is absolutely essential to keep the fermenting must in the optimum temperature. Yeast cells *will* ferment in an ordinary household refrigerator at a temperature of about 40° F. (5° C.) and also up to a temperature of 100° F. (38° C), over which they are killed, but the cells are not at their best in these circumstances. Experiment has shown time and again that they function best at a temperature between 60° F. and 75° F. (16-24° C.). The energy released in fermentation raises the temperature a few degrees, so you should take care not to allow the must to get too hot.

The importance of temperature during fermentation cannot be overstressed. The ferment can cease if the temperature rises too high or falls too low. Sometimes this cessation is only temporary and the ferment can be restarted by moving the vessel into a cooler or a warmer place. But frequently a "stuck" ferment can be very difficult to start again.

To ensure this equilibrium of temperature many winemakers now resort to a thermostatically controlled fermentation cupboard, where the temperature remains regulated for as long as required. With the frequent and often sudden variations in atmospheric temperature which we experience, in Great Britain at least, the advantages of such a cupboard are manifest.

On the other hand yeast cells are reasonably tolerant of some variation and it is not difficult to find some place in the house where a fairly steady temperature prevails. Often there are a few square feet of floor space near the kitchen stove, or the furnace, or there may be a square shelf in a cupboard. It is worth while making a careful survey to find the best spot to use for fermentation.

A few hours after adding an actively fermenting yeast starter

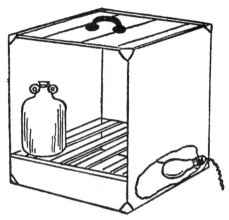

Fig 14   Fermentation cupboard, made from a tea chest. The heater or bulb, shown here at the side for convenience, should be fixed in the centre of the floor

to the must, carbon dioxide will begin to pass through the air-lock in the form of bubbles. For the first few days, the yeast will reproduce itself by using the oxygen dissolved in the must, rather than that in the sugar. Very little alcohol is formed in this period, when a great number of yeast cells are produced. Sometimes there is frothing, especially if there is much pectin present, and that is why it is as well not to fill the fermentation jar too full during this early period. After a few days the pectinase, either in its natural form or in the form of Pectozyme, will have dissolved the pectin which will even then begin to settle as sludge. Further, the yeast will have absorbed all the free oxygen and, provided we cut off its air supply by using an air-lock, it will have to turn to the sugar for further supplies. During this next period of fermentation much alcohol will be formed, although the conditions are not suitable for the production of many more yeast cells. The fermentation will not, and indeed should not, now be vigorous. It may be so apparently slow that you can only see a tiny ring of bubbles around the rim of the must. This is all to the good and is the best fermentation of all. The sugar will steadily be converted into alcohol and carbon dioxide without losing any of the natural aroma of the ingredient concerned.

It has been taken for granted in this chapter that an air-lock of some sort will be used. They are now readily available and their use is widely and well understood. Not only will all the air and its impurities be kept out of the must, but the very exclusion of the air, which of course contains oxygen, forces the yeast to turn to the sugar for its oxygen supply. The air-lock thus has positive as well as negative values. It is virtually impossible to make a dry wine or one very strong in alcohol without an air-lock. Its importance as the winemaker's best friend can never be over-emphasized.

It has also been taken for granted that a yeast nutrient will have been added to the must prior to the addition of the yeast. Once again, it is virtually impossible to make a dry wine or one strong in alcohol without the assistance given to the yeast by some form of nutrient.

The must may possibly ferment for several months and all this time the temperature should be kept as even as possible. Sometimes, unfortunately, the bubbles cease to rise within 3 or 4 weeks and to all intents and purposes the fermentations is finished. This is where the hydrometer proves so useful and a check on the specific gravity will give precise information as to the situation in the must. If the readings show a drop of 100 or more degrees it is likely that the fermentation is nearing its end. The alcoholic content of the wine will be reaching a point near the limit of toleration by the yeast. The yeast will soon be completely inhibited by the quantity of alcohol in the wine and will be unable to ferment any remaining sugar. This again emphasizes the danger of adding too much sugar at the start. Since the yeast can take no further action, it slowly sinks to the bottom of the vessel, together with the tartaric acid which the alcohol has converted to cream of tartar. Sometimes these crystals can be very clearly seen adhering to the jar.

But what if the hydrometer reading shows a reduction in gravity of only 40° to 50°? Providing there is plenty of sugar left in solution, then clearly the fermentation has "stuck", i.e. for some reason the yeast has temporarily stopped its activity. A situation has arisen in which the yeast is unable to reproduce itself, unable to live its normal life.

There are a number of possible causes and remedies and there are some still unknown. The known causes will be discussed first. There are seven of them altogether, but the first of these has already been mentioned—the natural conclusion to fermentation by the alcoholic inhibition of the yeast. Whether the wine is sweet or dry it is at least strong, or rather, at least as strong as the yeast you are using can make it. It may be that a different yeast would ferment on for a few more degrees, but that is a lesson to be learnt for another wine. It is too late to do anything about that now. You have a fully fermented wine and it should now be racked and matured.

Oddly enough, sugar is the next possible cause of cessation of ferment. Possibly you added so much to begin with that the yeast has been oppressed by the quantity present. Remember that sugar is often used as a preservative and if you have used too much then you are "preserving" your must. The best remedy here is to make up a quantity of similar must, *but without sugar,* and mix the two together, giving them a thorough aeration in the process. If this is not possible, dilute the must with water and lemon juice. An initial specific gravity in the region of 1·150 is an indication that too much sugar may be the cause of non-fermentation.

Similarly, if too small a quantity of sugar is used to start with, and more has not been added since, it may have all fermented and the yeast ceased activity for want of an oxygen source. The remedy naturally lies in adding sugar to the must. . . . This is not a common cause of a "stuck" ferment and usually arises from an intention to add additional sugar during fermentation, and forgetting to do so.

If you are not using an orthodox air-lock and the carbon dioxide is unable to escape easily, especially if for some reason, perhaps beyond your control, you are fermenting at a low temperature, it may be that the carbon dioxide dissolved in the must-cum-wine is inhibiting the activity of the yeast. The solution here is fairly simple. Remove the air-lock, give the wine a very good stir, allowing for a good deal of frothing in the process. In addition to getting rid of the excessive carbon dioxide, the wine will be oxygenated and a fresh crop of yeast cells will grow and continue the fermentation. One can achieve the same result by pouring the liquid from one container to another from a height. Don't forget to replace the fermentation trap and put the jar back into a warm place.

The remaining reasons for a stopped fermentation are fairly obvious ones. Has the yeast used up all the nutrient? Did you add sufficient at the beginning? If you did not, then it is probably too late now to do anything. Simply adding nutrient at this stage rarely has any effect. Sometimes it is possible to re-start the ferment by taking out half a pint of the liquid, adding some nutrient and fresh yeast to it and allowing this to get under way as a fresh "starter" before adding it to the bulk of the wine. Tronozymol or other good yeast energizer is the best nutrient to use now.

It is often helpful in these circumstances if, instead of adding the half-pint starter to say a gallon of must, the half-pint is first added to another half-pint. When this is fermenting well, add this pint to another pint, when the quart is well away add it to another quart, and so on, until all the wine is mixed in. But much trouble can be saved by making sure that the yeast has plenty of nutrient at the very beginning. If you are ever in doubt it is safest to err on the side of generosity as far as nutrient is concerned.

Acid is the next culprit. The yeast needs acid, particularly citric acid, and cannot ferment adequately without it. If when the fermentation sticks, you remember that you forgot to add the necessary quantity of citric acid during the preparation of the must, then it isn't too late now. Perhaps you did add the juice of a lemon, but maybe it wasn't large enough or juicy enough for the purpose. Add some more now, give the wine a thorough aeration and hope for the best. If it doesn't start again, adopt the method suggested above and prepare a fresh starter.

Finally we come back to temperature again. If the must has got too hot the yeast may all have died. It cannot live at all in a temperature above 105° F. (41° C.) and is certainly unhappy and ailing above 80° F. (27° C.). Move the fermenting vessel into a cooler—but not a cold—place and if necessary prepare a fresh starter. On the other hand if the wine has been left in an unheated room, in winter, then the yeast has "hibernated". Happily fermentation usually begins again without much difficulty when the jar is placed in a warm room for a few days.

These are the reasons known at present to cause temporary cessation of fermentation. Sometimes, however, a ferment will stick and none of the remedies recommended will start it again. It will obstinately remain apparently lifeless, perhaps for months, and then for no reason that you can explain, fermentation will begin again of its own volition. For this reason a "stuck" must should be kept under observation even in storage. It may one day blow its cork and start fermenting gently. Be thankful, and pop an air-lock into the neck of the jar!

Mention was made earlier about adding sugar during the fermentation, and this method has many advantages. Apart from ensuring a really satisfactory ferment, the yeast seems to be able to ferment on to a higher alcoholic tolerance than usual. If you are trying to make a really strong wine, then this is undoubtedly the best possible method to adopt.

A hydrometer is a great help with this method, for with its help you can keep accurate records of the progress of the fermentation. No complicated mathematics are involved. First check the specific gravity of the must without any sugar, and make a note of the reading. Then decide on the total amount of sugar you will need to give you the results you desire. You will find the table in the chapter on the Hydrometer helpful to you in this connection.

For example, to produce a medium sweet wine with an alcohol content of about 16% by volume.

Specific gravity of must without added sugar—1·030. (We see from the table on page 63 that this is equivalent to ½ lb. of sugar in an Imperial gallon of must).

From further reference to the table you can see that a specific gravity of 1·130 if fermented to dryness will produce just over 17% of alcohol, which is about as much as you can hope for, even with a good yeast.

A specific gravity of 1·130 is equivalent to about 3 lbs. of sugar in an Imperial gallon of must, and as there is ½ lb. already in our example, then we only need an additional 2½ lbs.

This will occupy a space equivalent to 1¾ Imperial pts. and so sufficient space should be left for it in the fermenting jar.
Start off by adding 1 lb. of dry sugar to the 6¾ Imperial pts. of must and stir till it is dissolved, before adding the yeast and starting the ferment. The 1 lb. of sugar will have raised the specific gravity to about 1·068 which in a few days will have been reduced by fermentation to about 1·020.

When the gravity has been reduced as suggested, remove the air-lock, take out some wine and dissolve in it say ¾ lb. of sugar, pour this slowly into the jar in case there is a frothing and replace the air-lock. The specific gravity will now be up to about 1·050 and fermentation should continue unabated.

There is only ¾ lb. of sugar left to add now, and it is recommended that this be added in 4-oz. lots, each time the specific gravity falls to 1·010. Each time take out a little of the wine, dissolve the sugar in it and pour it slowly and carefully back into the wine. Provided the must had plenty of acid and nutrient in it and you used a wine yeast, and provided you have kept the jar in a nice warm place all the time, the fermentation may continue to dryness and you will have an extremely strong wine. It may, however, cease during the fermentation of the last 4 ozs. of sugar and leave you with a final specific gravity somewhere about 1·010. A medium sweet wine of excellent strength that should be racked and matured for a year or so and will keep for many years, though human nature being what it is, this is unlikely!

If the wine isn't quite sweet enough for your liking, then a little more sugar may be added; 2 ozs. to the Imperial gallon will be found plenty. Once more the advantages of not using too much sugar are exemplified. Only 2½ lbs. of sugar have been used with an average must to produce a really strong wine. And what is the most important is that the result is no more than medium sweet wine. Imagine what 4 lbs. of sugar would have produced—little more than a slightly alcoholic cordial!

The technique of fermentation, then, may be summed up as follows:

1. Make sure that there is sufficient acid in your must.
2. Make sure there is sufficient nutrient in your must.
3. Don't use too much sugar. Remember that the best results are obtained by adding sugar during fermentation.
4. Use a good yeast already activated.
5. Stand your vessel in an even temperature between 60° F. and 75° F. (16 – 24° C.).
6. Rack as soon as fermentation finishes.

Chapter 14

RACKING

RACKING SIMPLY means the removal of clear, or clearing, wine from the deposit of lees at the bottom of the fermentation or storage jar.

When fermentation of any wine is nearing cessation the moving clouds of yeast cells, cream of tartar, dissolved pectin and so on will begin to settle and the wine will start to clear. In the normal way this is the moment to "rack" for the first time. The "normal way", because sometimes you can rack a little sooner if you want to reduce the quantity of yeast and try to stop the fermentation while the wine is still sweet and before too much alcohol is formed. Racking removes the insoluble particles from wine, helps it to clear and also helps to stabilize it before storing. Failure to rack at the end of fermentation could spoil your wine disastrously.

After a yeast cell has budded some thirty times or so it dies a natural death. The cell then undergoes autolysis and subsequently decomposes. Some of these parts feed the remaining yeast, but the other parts—the nitrogenous ones—are less beneficial. When the number of autolysed cells form the major part of the deposit, then the nitrogenous particles impart a flavour of "decomposition" to the wine and give it a "musty" taste. Hence, remove the deposit and throw it away. Never use this to start another ferment.

After this first racking, some live cells remain suspended in the wine, but if the alcohol content is higher than the yeast can tolerate then these cells will sink to the bottom of the jar and may be removed at a second racking, some 3 or 4 months after the first. Being mostly live cells they may be used to start another ferment if you so wish.

Racking has another and important benefit to contribute to the process of maturation. Wine matured in a cask is able to absorb a small amount of air through the pores of the wood. The air is thoroughly filtered in the process and reaches the wine in a perfectly pure state. This small amount of air contains oxygen, which combines with the alcohol and aldehydes to form acids, which react further with alcohol to form esters. This is the action which matures and mellows a wine. Nowadays, however, most winemakers use glass or earthenware storage jars and of course these containers, being non-porous, prevent the entry of air. When we rack a wine from one jar to another, either by pouring it through a funnel, or, better, by siphoning it through a rubber tube, the wine comes into direct contact with the air for a few seconds. In these moments some air is absorbed by the wine and the oxygen is able to combine with the alcohol and aldehydes as described. Not too much air is required and racking every 3 or 4 months seems to provide just enough. Racking, then, not only eliminates undesirable waste matter but admits the entry of beneficial oxygen.

Rack for the first time when fermentation ends and again 3 or 4 months later unless a heavy deposit has been thrown earlier. If it has, then rack as soon as you notice it. Rack preferably by siphoning. Simply stand the jar of wine on a table and a clean empty jar on a chair directly beneath the wine. Insert a rubber tube into the jar of wine, suck the wine through the tube, pinch the end, put it into the empty jar and watch gravity do the work for you. It is an advantage to use a glass U-tube on the end of the rubber in the wine so that the wine is first sucked *down* into the tube, rather than *up*. Sometimes the force of the wine coming straight up into the tube pulls up and disturbs the deposit, which is just what you are trying to prevent.

You can also tie your rubber tube to a nonmetallic knitting needle, allowing the needle to touch the bottom of the jar and to project beyond the tube for a couple of inches. As the wine gets lower in the jar, tilt it gently sideways so that the depth of wine above the sediment is maintained.

After storage the wine is again racked, this time usually into bottles. It can safely be said that a wine should be racked at least three times, and more if the deposit requires it.

Each time a jar of wine is racked into another jar, some wine will be lost—however little. It is important to make up this loss by topping up the second jar, preferably from the excess quantity made. If there is no spare you can alternatively use a little of last year's wine of this type, if you have some. If this is not available you can use either plain cold boiled water, if the wine is sweet, or a weak solution of sugar and water if the wine is dry.

Chapter 15

HOW TO MAKE A TYPICAL WINE

Winemaking is fundamentally simple. As has been said in other parts of this book, wine has been made for perhaps 10,000 years and few of those who made wine in years gone by had the advantage of an education such as we all enjoy today. The few and easy operations were taught by parents to children who no doubt often rendered assistance, so learning at first hand while still young. With our increasing knowledge of scientific methods we have introduced safeguards and refinements that greatly help to maintain a fairly high standard from year to year. These details we have tried to explain as simply as we can, but in case there are some who feel confused, we have thought it useful to describe the making of a typical wine.

We have chosen gooseberry wine because the method used applies to so many other wines. See page 188 for a detailed ingredient list.

The best gooseberries for making wine are the small, hard, green berries that are available early in the season. But soft, pale green or golden berries may be used, though these develop a distinctive gooseberry flavour in the wine. If you decide to use these berries, it is suggested that you should make them into a sweet wine of fairly high alcoholic content and use it for dessert purposes.

Top and tail 6 lbs. of berries, place them in a polyethylene bucket and pour over them 1 Imperial gallon of boiling water. This will kill any wild yeasts or bacteria that may be adhering to the skins and will also soften the berries and begin to draw out their flavour. Cover with a polyethylene sheet held down with an elastic band, to keep out dust and germs, and leave to stand overnight. Next day, after rolling up your sleeves and washing your hands, crush each berry between your fingers. They pop easily and the inner goodness can then get out. It is better to do this than to cut the berries beforehand, since this way the seeds are not broken. If they were, their bitterness would spoil the wine. To be on the safe side, one Campden tablet may now be added to the mash, especially if the fruit was fully ripe, but if your fruit was hard and sour this should not be necessary. Be sure to re-cover the pail and put it aside for another two days.

After 2 days, remove the sheet and strain the mashed gooseberries and liquid through a nylon sieve or a stout linen cloth. Use your press to extract the last of the juice from the berries or,

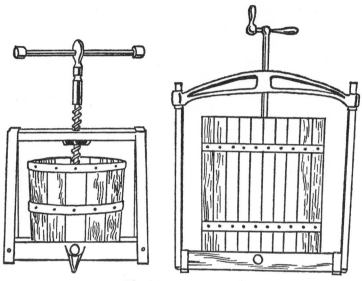

Fig 15   Fruit presses

having your berries in a strong cloth, twist and squeeze them until the juice ceases to flow.

Adjust your must as necessary by the addition of sugar, tannin and nutrients. Then finally add your yeast to begin the fermentation.

If the must has been prepared from green berries, it will, by the nature of the fruit, contain plenty of acid. If the berries were very ripe and sweet, then the juice of one lemon should be added. You should also add a ½ teaspoonful of grape tannin or a tablespoon of strong tea. One tablet or teaspoonful of yeast nutrient will be sufficient (depending on which proprietary brand you choose) for the Imperial gallon of must, and you can decide how much sugar to use in the light of the yeast starter already prepared and the quality of the original berries. For the green berries use 2½ lbs. of sugar—enough to give a specific gravity reading of 1·095—for they will have little natural sugar and this quantity will ferment to dryness and produce a table wine of about 12% - 13% alcohol. For very ripe berries, 3 lbs. of sugar (enough for an S.G. reading of 1·120) will also be sufficient to start with, and a further 4 ozs. can be added in 2 weeks' time and a final 4 ozs. a week after that. This should produce a wine containing 15% or 16% alcohol, and with a small residue of sugar in solution sufficient to make the wine taste sweet.

For the green berries, an all-purpose wine yeast may be used, or as an alternative a burgundy yeast, which in these circumstances will produce a table wine resembling Chablis. This will be excellent with roast duck or goose or halibut.

For the ripe and golden berries, a Sauterne yeast is recommended.

When the preparation of the must is complete, transfer it to a clean dry fermentation jar, insert the fermentation trap and stand the jar in a warm place so that a temperature of 60° – 75° F.) 16 – 24° C.) can be maintained. In the first instance don't fill the jar but rather use two jars so that the vigorous fermentation won't work into the trap and perhaps overflow. When the tumult has died away, remove the fermentation traps, transfer the contents of one jar to the other, reinsert a fermentation trap and continue to ferment as long as possible. The small amount of excess should be put into a bottle with a plug of cotton wool in the neck and stood beside the jar. Fermentation should continue steadily for several weeks more. When fermentation has quite finished and no more bubbles of carbon dioxide can be seen rising in the jar or passing through the fermentation trap, the wine will begin to clear and as much as ¼ in. of sediment may be deposited on the bottom of the jar. This is the time to rack the wine carefully into a fresh jar— checked for cleanliness of course—and to top up from the half-pint or so in the bottle.

Cork the jar firmly; make sure that it is labelled and store it in some cool dark place for 6 months. By that time the wine should have thrown a further deposit consisting mainly of inhibited yeast cells. This deposit may be used to make a yeast starter for other wines if you so wish.

Test for stability by standing half a glassful in the open room, and if the wine tends to brown, then add one Campden tablet to the jar. If there is no change in the colour, then there is no need for a tablet.

The time for bottling has now come, and for each Imperial gallon jar you should prepare six clean, dry, punted, clear glass bottles and six sound corks. A U.S. gallon will need five bottles and corks. Soften the corks by warming them to about 110° F. (44° C.) in a 10% solution of glycerine and water. When all is ready, remove the cork from the jar. If the wine has not cleared to brilliance, it should be filtered or fined in any way you choose, as indicated elsewhere in this book. Assuming the wine is clear, extract a small quantity and taste it. If you decide that it is too dry for you add, say, two teaspoonfuls of sugar to one of the bottles, fill it with wine, cork and shake till the sugar is dissolved and then taste it again, adding more sugar if necessary until you feel satisfied. Most likely, however, this will not be necessary.

Now siphon off into the bottles, filling each one to within 1½ ins. of the top of the neck. Cork the bottles tightly with whatever facilities you possess, whether it be a corking machine or simply a piece of plastic-covered wire. Fix a suitably coloured plastic capsule over each cork and neck, label the bottles and return to storage, laying the bottles on their side to finish maturing for a further 3 months at least.

When you begin to make gooseberry wine again is the time to start drinking your previous vintage. If all has gone well, the green berries will provide you with a fine table wine—possibly even sparkling. It should be served well chilled from a decanter into goblet glasses. If you have used ripe golden berries, the wine may still need further time to mature and it is recommended that you leave it in storage till Christmas. Then decant it and serve it as a dessert wine.

Note: Bottles originally made to hold hard liquor should not be used for bottling wines. If further fermentation occurs, they could explode—with very, very grave results if you happened to be holding them up to the light at the time.

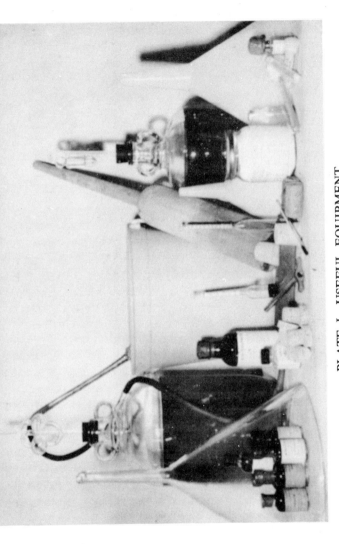

PLATE I   USEFUL EQUIPMENT

At the back (l to r), a 1-gallon glass jar with rubber stopper and fermentation lock, a siphon made from glass and rubber tubing, a polyethylene bucket, a wooden "masher", a ½-gallon glass jar and lock. In front (l to r), a large funnel suitable for filtering, bottles of Fermenta flavourings, sulphite, two hydrometers, a cork borer and corks, a thermometer, two polyethylene funnels, a jar of Tronozymol yeast nutrient, a selection of wine yeasts.

PLATE II TYPES OF YEAST

At the back (l to r), Heath and Heather granulated packed yeast, a bottle culture, Fermenta liquid yeast, a Kitzinger yeast; front (l to r), baker's yeast, Fermenta yeast tablets, a Grey Owl laboratories tube culture on agar, and a Liofermenti dried yeast.

PLATE III   HANDY CONTAINERS

Left to right, 2-gallon, 1-gallon stone jars, a 3-gallon cask, a 1-gallon glass jar, a Winchester, a ½-gallon glass jar, a 5-gallon white cylindrical crock and a 5-gallon "breadbin" crock. The last two are useful for the initial soaking period.

PLATE IV   TYPES OF FERMENTATION LOCK

Left to right, the neat German "Hobby" lock, the Sherrard Semplex lock (both virtually unbreakable) and two types of glass lock.

PLATE V   RACKING BY MEANS OF A SIPHON

A slit must be cut down the side of the cork to allow air to enter the jar, and the glass tube must be a loose fit in the cork so that it can gradually be pushed lower and lower.

PLATE VI FILTERING WITH ASBESTOS PULP

In the funnel, from bottom to top, are: a plug of cotton wool, a handful of asbestos pulp, a saucer and the uncleared wine. If the apparatus is to be left for some time unattended, it is as well to cover it with a cloth and to put a little cotton wool around the neck of the funnel inside the neck of the jar. This keeps out the vinegar flies.

PLATE VII WINE GLASSES

Left to right: general-purpose wine glass for medium strength wines and cocktails; hock; sherry; port; champagne; liqueur; a useful general-purpose goblet; small and large Parisian goblets. The glass should be only half filled, as shown, so that the narrowing upper portion will retain the bouquet.

PLATE VIII   THE FINISHED PRODUCT

Chapter 16

SPECIAL WINE TYPES

IN CONSIDERING the special wine types which amateurs may wish to imitate, it is necessary to mention that the originals are all made from grape wines, usually with something added. At one time the additions of aromatic herbs and spices were perhaps intended to conceal a poor wine. It was also discovered that a quantity of alcohol added to a wine not only improved its flavour but enabled the wine to be transported over long distances, with consequent vibrations, and yet still be sound when it reaches its destination.

Over the years different wines have emerged as distinctive types. The best known, in England at least, are of course port and sherry, but there are numerous others including champagne, vermouth, aperitifs and liqueurs, to mention only a few.

PORT WINE

The name Port, as everyone knows, may only be applied to that wine fermented from the juice of the grapes grown on the banks of the River Douro, fortified with grape alcohol and shipped through the city of Oporto. In many parts of the world, notably in Australia, an excellent wine of remarkable similarity to port, for all but the rare connoisseur, can be, and is, made year after year without failures due to bad weather. To protect the original wine, the vintners and shippers concerned with the Portuguese wine have "patented" their name as it were, and now they alone may call their wine "port". Similar wine made in other parts of the world must be called "port type".

From suitable ingredients, we too can make a "port type" wine. Blackberries, elderberries and particularly damsons are perfectly suitable.

It is necessary to ferment these wines as long as possible, to the highest degree of alcohol content attainable, so that only the minimum quantity of expensive alcohol need be added. It is recommended that 2½ lbs. of sugar per Imperial gallon be used at first, or, if you use a hydrometer, a must with a specific gravity of 1·100. As this ferments towards dryness add more sugar at the rate of, say, 4 ozs. each week for 3 weeks, or with a hydrometer when the S.G. reaches 1·015 raise it again to 30, and so on until the yeast is totally inhibited and fermentation finishes completely, even in a warm atmosphere of say 75° - 80° F. The final specific gravity should be in the region of 1·010 and the wine should have an alcoholic content of perhaps 17%. By keeping careful note of the *total* reduction in specific gravity it is possible to calculate the approximate quantity of alcohol present. Sufficient extra alcohol, according to the figure obtained from using the Pearson Square (see page 117, may then be added to bring the wine up to an approximate alcoholic content of 20%. It need hardly be said that you must use a port wine yeast because this has been cultured from the yeast growing on the grapes from which real port wine is made. This yeast is responsible for much of the flavour of port and that is why port type wine can be made in so many parts of the world. Soil and climatic conditions play a fundamental part, however, and for this reason the wine from Oporto, although often imitated, is never equalled.

If you fortify your wine it will keep for many years, but it is doubtful if it will improve much beyond three years, though it will certainly take at least a year before it is drinkable at all.

This imitation port wine should be treated with exactly the same care as you would treat a good real port wine. It will continue to throw a deposit while it is in bottle and so should be handled with care, and be decanted in such a way before serving as not to disturb the lees. It is a dessert wine and should therefore be drunk alone, say with a slice of fruit cake, or after dinner, and of course it should be served at room temperature, i.e. about 70° F.

Among the extracts that you can buy is one called Prunelle and this added to a bottle of damson wine fermented with a port yeast, but unfortified, will give an excellent imitation of a good port. In Portugal about a fifth of the total grape alcohol to be used is added when the wine is pressed—usually a couple of days after the grapes are trodden and broken and therefore soon after fermentation has started. This inhibits the fermentation and consequently a long slow ferment is induced, and the remaining fortification is carried out at subsequent intervals. The wine remains in cask for at least two years.

Dry white and dry red ports are made as well as sweet red ports, and this presents no special problems to the imitator. For white port use a white must made from any of a great variety of fruits and roots not too strong in flavour or body, ferment with a port yeast to dryness and the highest alcoholic content attainable by careful judgment based on hydrometer readings. A dry red port is made similarly, but with the same must as for sweet red port.

SHERRY

In Southern Spain, in the country around the little town of Jerez, a fine wine is made from white grapes in a unique manner, and is fortified *after* the fermentation is complete. As port takes its name from the town of Oporto so sherry takes its name from the town of Jerez — pronounced Hereth. The distinctive feature of sherry is that it is fermented ultimately in the presence of air, by several different strains of saccharomyces ellipsoideus indigenous to the grapes grown in that area. One of the strains grows only on the surface of the wine where it is in contact with the air and forms a firm, crinkly, creamy skin called "flor". This yeast can live in a higher concentration of alcohol than other strains and gives a delightful flavour to the wine, by fermenting sugar and alcohol into aldehydes and even more complex substances. There is little danger of the wines being attacked by the mycoderma aceti, because the must is well "plastered" with calcium sulphate (gypsum) to increase the acidity, a condition disliked by the vinegar bacillus.

Wines resembling sherry can be made at home from a must prepared from apples, Victoria plums, rhubarb and so on, provided a sherry yeast is used, and instead of sealing the fermentation trap with water, the trap is left open and the open end lightly plugged with *un*medicated cotton wool. This prevents vinegar flies from obtaining access, but enables carbon dioxide to escape and pure air to enter. The wine should be racked at the end of the tumultuous ferment, say in 10 days, but a slow ferment will then begin and continue perhaps for 6 months. The wine should not be racked during this period so as not to remove the yeast cells still converting the sugar into alcohol. Unfortunately the formation of the yeast film on the must at home is by no means certain, but the wine will eventually clear by itself and should possess the distinctive sherry flavour. It may be fortified to 18% alcohol if you wish.

Sherry can be made either sweet or dry and fine or rich. Usually one makes a fine dry sherry or a sweet rich sherry. For a fine dry sherry use a must with not too much body such as white cherry, or gooseberry or rhubarb, and use white sugar.

As usual start off with 2½ lbs. per Imperial gallon and add two lots of 4 ozs. in successive weeks, finishing with dryness. For a sweet rich sherry similar to an Oloroso or a brown add 1 lb. of wheat to the must, which could be of apple or Victoria plum. This gives additional body to the wine. Start off with 3 lbs. sugar per Imperial gallon and again add two lots of 4 ozs.

in successive weeks. If the wine finishes a little dry another ounce or two of sugar may be added to taste.

It is customary to serve fine dry sherry quite cold (but not glacé) as an aperitif and sweet rich sherries as dessert wines.

With the aid of one good sherry yeast culture you can make a suitable starter that you can divide from time to time and during a season make a variety of sherries from differents musts ranging from a fine dry through graduations of sweetness and richness to an Oloroso. Sherry flavourings to add to a finished wine (e.g. rhubarb) can also now be obtained.

CHAMPAGNE

Commercially this wine needs more attention than almost any other wine and is accordingly more expensive. The wine is bottled when fermentation is almost complete and the bottles are stood nearly upside down, so that further deposits are thrown on to the cork. The bottles are frequently twisted to shake deposits from the sides of the bottle on to the cork, and the bottle is gradually stood more upright until the vertical is eventually reached. When the wine is judged to be quite dry the cork is removed, the pressure ejects the deposit, the bottle is returned to the upright, a small quantity of wine syrup is added to fill the bottle and a new cork is driven home. In modern champagne cellars the necks are frozen so that no wine escapes and the icy deposit is withdrawn with the cork. The wine syrup is fermented by the remaining enzymes, the carbon dioxide so formed is dissolved but escapes in bubbles when the bottle is opened and the wine poured into broad shallow glasses, which show off this sparkle to good effect, or tulip glasses, which retain the sparkle much longer.

In making a sparkling wine resembling champagne, then, use a white must, preferably apples, as their flavour resembles that of champagne. Use of course a champagne yeast, ferment with 2½ lbs. to 3 lbs. of white sugar per Imperial gallon for a dry or semi-dry wine as required, rack several times after fermentation is finished till the wine is brillant, then bottle, adding a tablespoonful of sugar dissolved in a little wine to each bottle, and wire on the corks. Store in a cool place and keep for a year. Then serve—well chilled—with ice chips in a surrounding ice bucket. The chilling is important as it helps to keep the carbon dioxide in the wine so that it escapes steadily rather than with a rush.

VERMOUTH

A low aromatic shrub grows in Britain as well as in many other parts of the world. We call it wormwood; the French call it Vermouth. It is the principal but by no means the only herb used in flavouring this fortified wine—for in addition to herbs, alcohol is added till the wine contains 20% alcohol by volume. You can buy a packet of mixed herbs including wormwood. You can buy an extract of these herbs and you can also buy a variety of herbs and make up your own individual concoction. There are basically two vermouths, sweet and dry. The sweet is usually darker in colour and richer in body with an alcoholic content of about 18%. The dry is lighter in colour and in body and a little stronger—20% alcohol.

You may choose your herbs from among balm, gentian, yarrow, angelica, chamomile, cinnamon, cloves, nutmeg, coriander and so on. The essential for 1 Imperial gallon of wine is 2 ozs. of wormwood, ½ oz. of balm and ½ oz. of yarrow and as little as ⅛ oz. of gentian, angelica and chamomile with just traces of cinnamon, clove, nutmeg, etc. Increase the quantities in accordance with the quantity of wine to be treated. Put the herbs in a cotton bag and soak them in some strong wine for 2 or 3 days to extract the flavouring. Add this essence to the wine to be treated. Any undistinguished wine will do or you can make one specially for the purpose, such as tea wine or unflavoured rice wine. It is as well to increase the alcoholic content of the wine first and then to add the essence gradually until all is included or until the wine has attained a flavour to suit your palate.

The wine should be served alone, since the strong flavour would not mix well with others, or better still with gin.

LIQUEURS

Most liqueurs have a very high alcoholic content and usually consist of grape alcohol flavoured with essences of berries, roots, herbs, spices and so on. Certain information is given in the chapter on Blending for the use of extracts, but you may wish to try your hand at cherry brandy, sloe gin and the like. For cherry brandy use morello cherries, ripe to the point of red-black. Pick out the stalks, or if you like a slightly bitter drink, cut them in half, prick the cherries with a needle to allow the juice to flow and steep them in sweetened brandy for 6 months in a well-sealed bottle or jar.

For example—use 1 lb. of morello cherries, ½ lb. of sugar and a bottle of brandy. At the end of 6 months strain off the liqueur into a fresh bottle, cork but use as soon as required. The cherries are excellent in trifles or fruit flan.

Sloe gin is made similarly, but you cannot buy the sloes and must pick them from the hedges when you can find them. To 1 lb. of sloes add 3 ozs. of sugar and a bottle of gin. Wash and prick the sloes first, add the sugar and gin, cork securely, shake to dissolve the sugar and store for a year. Strain off the sloes and bottle your liqueur for use when and as required.

Similarly you can make apricot brandy, peach brandy, pineapple brandy, and so on.

As these liqueurs are strong, rich and sweet they should be served sparingly at the end of a meal; beforehand they would cloy the palate.

OTHER WINE TYPES

With suitable musts as well as with the appropriate yeast cultures you can make wines resembling burgundy both white and red, Sauternes, Tokay and so on. It would be tedious to go into greater detail but naturally you must use a white "must" with good body and only 2½ lbs. of sugar to the Imperial gallon to make a Chablis, which is a dry white burgundy. For Sauternes and Tokay a similar white must with even more body should be used. Include 1 lb. of wheat, rice or other cereal and 3½ lbs. of sugar per Imperial gallon. A must with a good natural bouquet is also helpful here. For a red burgundy use a red must such as red and black currants in the proportion of 3 lbs. red to 1 lb. black, with 1 lb. of cereal and 3 lbs. sugar. With thought and care based on experience you can imitate a great many wine types quite successfully.

Chapter 17
CELLARCRAFT

THE PROBLEM of maturing wines quickly has long held the attention of those engaged professionally in making and selling wine. In America they talk of "ageing" the wine and in an endeavour to hurry the process they sometimes "cook" their wine for 2 or 3 months at a temperature of 140° F. (60° C.) and then freeze it to slush to remove the cream of tartar. They also add finings and filter under pressure several times, and then store their wine at what we regard as room temperature—65° F. (18° C.). Furthermore, they use vast vats made from redwood or concrete and sometimes pump pure air through the wine to obtain the benefits of oxidation. In France the wine is often matured in small oak casks containing 55 Imperial gals. which admit naturally the minute quantities of air required.

The home vintner is more often concerned with from 1 to 5 gals. and, in the normal course of racking, sufficient oxygen is usually taken up by the wine to ensure adequate maturation within a year or so. This is why our wines—even the best of them—are ready for drinking sooner than wines matured in much larger quantities.

Some "vin du pays" of France and Switzerland is consumed before it is one year old. This is wine made in relatively small quantities by individual peasants. Although some may be sold to the local café, most of it is served on the family table as part of a meal. So too with our wines!

There is a tendency to think that the most important part of winemaking is the preparation of the must and the actual fermentation and that little else really matters. This is far from being so. The preparation of the must, and its fermentation, is of course very important, but good wine can be utterly spoiled by bad cellarcraft and on the other hand a mediocre wine can be made to give of its best with proper care and attention.

For the purposes of this chapter, it is assumed that the wine has been fully fermented and is now ready for storage. First of all it must be thoroughly stirred and then allowed to settle down for a day or two. This not only ensures that fermentation is complete, but also releases dissolved carbon dioxide and admits a small quantity of air containing, of course, oxygen, which will combine with certain acids and alcohols to form adehydes and esters giving additional flavour and bouquet to the wine. This does not mean, however, that the greater the quantity of air admitted the better will be the wine. Too much air will certainly spoil the wine, even if it doesn't turn it to vinegar.

Some winemakers test for stability at this stage by standing a glass of the young wine in the open room for a few days. If the wine darkens because of oxidation one Campden tablet should be added to each gallon of wine as a stabilizer. The wine from the glass should *NOT* be returned to the jar after the experiment, but should be thrown away. If there is no change in the colour of the wine, then the bulk may be safely put into storage.

When the wine has had a chance to settle down after the stirring, and assuming that no more fermentation occurs, rack it off into a clean dry container. Moulds love moisture and a few cells may be in one of the drops, unless the jar has been freshly washed and rinsed. As the mould cells will multiply in the wine a bad flavour would gradually develop. If you are using barrels, or jars with taps, you will have no difficulty in racking, but remember not to shake up the sediment by carelessness when tilting. If you propose to siphon off the new wine, either use a glass tube with a U-bend at the end so that this protrudes above the sediment, or attach your glass or rubber tube to a bone or plastic knitting-needle about 1½ in. from the bottom, so that it does not accidentally slip into the lees. The new jar or barrel should be filled to the brim and corked tightly and a simple label attached to indicate the contents. The wine may taste young and raw but it will undergo subtle changes during the next 6 months or so and it may not then resemble the fruit or flower, etc., from which it was made.

During these months when the wine is maturing, it is best to store in a temperature of from 50° F. to 55° F. (10–13° C.). Ideally the cellar under the house is best, because the temperature there is little affected by external heat or cold. But some modern houses have no cellar and an alternative must be found. Seek a dark place, free from vibration and with an even temperature in both summer and winter.

Often floor boards can be sawn on the ground floor to reveal a crawl space perhaps 2 or 3 ft. deep and this makes a very useful store indeed. Or one would use the cupboard under the stairs, or cupboard on a north wall or some space in the larder. A brick-built garage or shed would also be suitable, but wooden ones tend to get rather hot in summer. If the chosen storage is likely to get very cold in winter, say 40° F. (5° C.) or less, then the wine should be covered with some insulating material to protect it from the extremes. Old newspapers, blankets, sacks, etc., are admirable for this purpose. These also serve to keep out the light which is harmful to maturing wines, especially red wines, which deposit their colour and fade.

If you are using even small casks, they will be both heavy and cumbersome, so it is worth while trying to store them in a place where they require the minimum of movement. You should be able to reach them easily and have room to insert a spile or a tap as well as being able to draw off when necessary. For this reason casks are best stored 12 to 18 ins. off the ground in a proper cradle, whether it is bought or made at home. Glass or glazed jars and plastic containers may be stood on the floor or a shelf and it is better to fill them to the cork, seal them, and store them upright than to risk laying them on their side. It is a tragedy to lose a gallon or more of wine because of one rolling jar hitting another, or even because of a blown cork.

If you have sufficient containers it is very well worth while maturing your wine in jars or barrels as long as possible. The increased volume enables the chemical changes to have more elbow room, as it were. Because of these changes, it is unwise to store wine in barrels smaller than 5 gals. and indeed 6 gals. is really small enough. The wood, being slightly porous, admits a small amount of air to the wine. A small amount is, as we have seen, beneficial but a large amount is deleterious. In a barrel the surface area of the wine in relation to its volume controls the amount of air actually admitted to the wine as a whole. The ratio between the surface area and the volume obviously decreases as the volume increases, so that the larger the barrel the smaller in proportion to the volume is the surface of wine exposed to the air through the porousness of the wood. Use, therefore, as big a barrel as you can and fill it full to the bung, or else use smaller non-porous containers. Do try, however, to mature your wines in bottle for some months as well.

It is very important to have a light in the store room and if possible this should be an unshaded electric light bulb—clear rather than pearl. If not, use a candle, securely fixed of course, where it cannot be knocked over. From time to time you will need to inspect your wine and experience has shown that it is better to hold it in front of the lights mentioned than any others. The clarity or otherwise of the wine will show to the best advantage.

After 3 or 4 months the wine may be tested again for stability as indicated and a bottle may be three parts filled, corked and stood in a warm place for a week to see whether any further fermentation occurs or deposit is thrown. If there are no reactions and if the wine is brilliantly clear it MAY now be bottled, though a further 3 months or so in jar will improve it still more.

If there are reactions then the wine obviously needs another Campden tablet to the gallon and further maturation.

Assuming that all is well and you decide to bottle, you will need six full-size, clean bottles for each Imperial gallon of wine. It is best to prepare the bottles beforehand, bearing in mind the remarks on this subject in the chapter on Hygiene.

Try if you can to use punted wine bottles, either clear or dark to suit the white or red wine you are bottling. The dark green bottle will protect the colour of your red wine. It is also worth while, especially if you have only a gallon of a certain wine, to use two or four half-size bottles in place of one or two full-size bottles. There may be occasions when half a bottle is sufficient for your needs and this will save opening a full bottle with the danger that the remaining half may deteriorate before it can be used.

Corks, too, should be got ready by warming them to about 110° F. (43° C.)—only just above blood heat—for some minutes, in a dilute solution of glycerine and water. This softens and sterilizes them safely. They should not be boiled as this adversely affects their quality and they are likely to stick in the neck of the bottle and have to be dug out. The weak glycerine solution helps to prevent greenish mould growth as well as to facilitate entry and withdrawal. Before use the corks should be stored in a cotton bag, keeping the new ones separate from the old—just in case!

The matured wine should be run into the bottles either from the tap or by siphon until it is about 2 ins. from the top of the bottle, and the cork should promptly be inserted. If you haven't a corking machine a piece of narrow-gauge plastic-covered wire wiped with a glycerine-impregnated wad of cotton wool should be inserted into the bottle before the cork. When the cork is being pushed right home the wire permits the air between the wine and the cork to escape so that there is no pressure under the cork to push it partially out again.

A plastic capsule appropriate to the colour of the wine can be put over the cork and neck of the bottle and as it dries it will form an efficient seal. Alternatively a metal foil may be used to cover the cork and this certainly adds lustre to the bottle if it is likely to be shown to other people. If you are bottling a champagne type of wine, it is desirable to wire the corks to the bottle, making sure that you obtain a firm grip over the cork.

The type of label you now put on the bottle is a matter of personal opinion, but you must put a label of some sort on if you have two wines of similar colour. If the wine is solely for your own use and you always serve it from a decanter anyway, then a small gummed label as used for home-made jams is enough. If you are likely to show the bottle to friends, or to give it away, or use it on your own table, then it is preferable to put a fancy label on the bottle with approximately equal distances above and below the label, but if anything a trifle higher rather than lower. This gives a better balance in appearance. It is important, too, to feel for the two seams of the bottle and to place the label between them, rather than over one of them. To do otherwise looks careless.

The bottles now being filled, corked, sealed and labelled are ready for storage and if they are to be kept for any length of

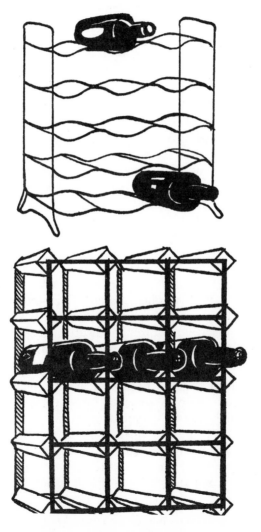

Fig 16 Types of wine rack

time they should be stored on their side in a rack bought or made for the purpose. It is best to store them label downwards, so that the label is less likely to become soiled by dust. If desired a small mark with white paint can be put on the shoulder of the bottle facing upwards and this spot should be kept in the same position all the time the bottle is in storage, so that any further sediment can collect in one place and not be disturbed. It is also a useful guide when removing the bottle from storage, prior to serving. Bottles may be stored upright if circumstances prevent storage in a rack, but they take rather more room that way and there is the danger that the cork will dry out and admit air to the wine (unless you are using polyethylene stoppers, which are excellent). With a plastic capsule, too, drying out is less likely, of course, and if the wine is only likely to remain in the bottle for a matter of a few months, the point is not so important. If you do store your bottles upright it is as well to store the wine in bulk for as long as possible, so that the period in bottle is reduced to the minimum.

The period of time necessary for maturing varies with the wine, but very few are really ready for drinking under 1 year from the time of making and fermenting; 6 months maturing in bulk and 3 months in bottle is a fair general guide. But even at 1 year a wine may not be quite ready and must then be kept for a while longer in cool dark storage. Indeed it is a worthwile experiment, if you can spare the wine, to put certain bottles aside for use in the more distant future. Very few home winemakers have ever had sufficient to save for more than 3 years, and unless the wines have been fortified with alcohol, or a must of a high specific gravity has fermented with a good yeast to form a high natural alcohol content, it is doubtful whether a wine made at home will improve very much beyond 3 years. It may indeed deteriorate through insufficient alcohol to begin with or through bad cellarcraft. As a general rule, the stronger the wine, the longer it will keep and should be kept.

In spite of all that has been said, it remains a fact that you can occasionally by-pass some of these operations. A wine of reasonably high alcohol content, say 13 - 14%, can be fermented in barrel and left on its lees to mature for 6 months and then drawn off into a decanter as required until the barrel is two-thirds empty. Then the last third is drawn off and bottled for use, though not stored. Note that it is not wise to leave too little in the cask.

The experienced winemaker may well know other "short cuts" or labour-saving devices that he personally uses with success.

Nevertheless a calculated risk is taken and the longest way is always the safest way for the less confident.

As soon as any bottles come into your possession, wash them thoroughly inside and out with warm water containing a little domestic bleach. This is wonderful for cleaning stained and dirty bottles, but rinse each bottle five or six times in clean fresh water afterwards. Stand the bottles upside down to drain and don't put them away until they are quite dry. It is best never to use bottles that have contained disinfectant or poisons. Don't cork the bottles during storage, in case they develop a musty odour, unless they contain sulphite solution. Either plug them with cotton wool, store them upside down, or cover them with a cloth. Before you fill them, they can be rinsed in a weak solution of sulphite equivalent to one Campden tablet to a gallon of warm water, and shaken to get out most of the drops. Sometimes you may receive bottles containing the dregs of the previous contents. Whether this be alcohol or wine always wash the bottles as suggested and never put your wine into the bottle hoping to improve the flavour or strength of your own wine.

Occasionally one comes across unusual bottles or jars and it is not always easy to know just how much they will contain. The following list might then be useful:

	Imperial			*Metric*
"Miniature"	1½	fluid oz.		45 ml.
"Quarter"	6½	"	"	190 ml.
½ pt (Imp.)	10	"	"	300 ml.
Half-bottle (wine)	13½	"	"	400 ml.
Pint (beer)	20	"	"	600 ml.
Punted wine bottle	26⅔	"	"	750 ml.
1 litre bottle (aperitif)	35½	"	"	1 litre
Quart cider or beer (Imp.) . . .	40	"	"	1·2 "
Large Chianti	63	"	"	1·8 "
2-litre Winchester	71	"	"	2 "
2-qt. Winchester	80	"	"	2·3 "
Large Winchester	100	"	"	3 "
1-gal. glass jar	170	"	"	5 "

If the bottle was opened carelessly and the cork was broken and pushed down into the wine, it must be removed before washing the bottle. Insert a loop of string into the bottle, which should then be inverted and jiggled about until the broken cork lies at the base of the neck of the bottle with the two ends of the string on either side. The secret is to pull, gently at first, gradually increasing the strain as the cork shows signs of coming out. On your side make sure that you don't break the cork when opening a bottle. Use a corkscrew with a wide screw and twist it in the centre of the cork, until the point shows through at the other end. If you do this carefully, you will have no difficulty in withdrawing the whole cork in one piece with a long steady pull.

Every winemaker would like to possess at least one barrel, but is put off, for a time at least, by the cost. Sooner or later, however, a present or a 'plunge" provides one and the question arises, how to prepare it for use.

It is as well to resist all offers of vinegar barrels, since the wood will be so impregnated with vinegar as to be beyond use for wine.

First of all examine the barrel carefully to see that it is not damaged in any way. Most likely the iron bands will already be painted, but if they are showing signs of rust they must be done again. Usually the bands are only knocked on and can as easily be knocked off with the aid of a blunt chisel and a mallet. It is most important not to take them all off at once. Take off two at a time, rub them down hard and paint with two coats of good quality bituminous enamel paint. When these two are dry, replace them and remove the other two, treating them similarly. Remove any old corks with a loop of string and then fill the barrel with clean water and leave it for 3 or 4 days to swell the timbers. Don't worry if at first there is a little seepage, this will disappear as the staves tighten together. Keep the cask on a rack, of course. After a few days empty out the water and half fill with boiling water in which ordinary washing soda has been dissolved in the proportion of 3 ozs. to the gallon of water. (20 grams per litre).

Put a new bung in the bung hole and hammer it in so that the hole is watertight. During the next half-hour roll the cask as vigorously as you can, with intervals for rests of course! Leave the cask to cool for an hour or so, then bang on the staves around the bung hole to release the bung, lift it out, empty the cask and rinse thoroughly several times. Now make up a solution of ¼ oz. of potassium metabisulphite and ¼ oz. of citric acid in a gallon of water—cold or hot (1½ grams each per litre). Pour this into the barrel, bung down and again roll it vigorously for several minutes, so that the solution can get into every possible part of the cask. Remove the bung as before, drain and thoroughly rinse, then drain again. The barrel is now ready for its first wine. Fill to the bung hole, bung down tight and store on a cradle. Don't forget to chalk the name of the wine above the tap hole.

Should you wish to find out whether the wine is ready for serving or bottling before tapping the barrel, a sample can be removed through the bung hole with the aid of a pipette or just a simple glass tube. Carefully remove the bung, and having sterilized the pipette or glass tube and shaken it dry, insert it slowly into the wine. Count to ten before removing it so that the wine can rise fully up the tube. Next place your forefinger over the end of the tube which you can hold between your middle finger and thumb. Press tightly with your forefinger to seal the end, lift out the tube, hold it over a glass and then lift your finger. The wine can now run freely into the glass.

When the time comes to tap the barrel, you will need a wooden tap about 4 to 6 ins. long. Soak it for a few minutes in a solution of ¼ oz. of potassium metabisulphite and ¼ oz. of citric acid per gallon, rinse and drain. Next fit a porous spile in the bung so that air can enter through the spile when the wine is drawn off. The wine will not otherwise flow, since to do so it would have to overcome a vacuum and this it could not do by natural gravity. Don't forget the porous spile plug, then. Now take the tap in your left hand and the mallet in your right. Place the neck of the tap which is to enter the barrel in the centre of the bung in the tap hole. You will find this in one end of the barrel near the side. Before tapping you should ensure that it is in central position, and at the bottom. Wipe it over with a cloth dipped in the solution mentioned. Take careful aim and give the head of the tap a smart blow with a mallet, sufficient to drive the bung into the wine and the tap into the hole all with the one blow. Just in case of bad luck it might be as well to have a clean bowl beneath to catch any drips. If you have had to move the barrel at all, you must now leave it to stand for 3 or 4 days for the sediment to settle, before withdrawing any wine. Having read this, take care that when you are storing your barrels you put them in such a position that they need not be moved at all, when the time comes to be tapped.

When the barrel is empty, remove the tap cork through the bung hole, which is large, and put a fresh cork or small bung in the tap hole before washing out the barrel prior to using again. If you have to store an empty barrel for some months, keep it filled with water in which six Campden tablets and ½ oz. of citric acid have been dissolved. Every 3 months empty and refill. If you prefer to use a potassium metabisulphite solution, then 1¼ ozs. should be dissolved in 1 Imp. qt. of water, 1 oz. in 1 U.S. quart or 35 grams per litre water, 1 fl. oz. or 25 ml. of this liquid is equivalent to two Campden tablets. Commercial preparations for cleaning dirty casks and containers and for keeping sweet those not in use can be obtained from your winemaking supply store.

Chapter 18
KEEPING RECORDS

O NE OF the most difficult tasks in making wine is to repeat successes. So very often you forget precisely what you did 12 or 15 months ago to a particular wine, especially if you have made a good number of other wines in between. In the same way, when a wine fails to come up to expectations, it is so difficult to remember just where you went wrong. The simple answer, of course, is to keep adequate records. But the very thought of getting out a book, finding a pen or pencil and jotting down the relevant facts is abhorrent to those many winemakers who do not possess a "Civil Service Mind". Perhaps in the not too far distant future one of the equipment firms will evolve a simple printed card, leaving just a few blank spaces for us to fill in.

In the meantime, try making a record card for yourself. A packet of ordinary 5" × 7" lined index cards will suffice most people for a season. Make a couple of holes in the top to take a short piece of string to form a loop to hang over the neck of the jar and prepare each card as follows or to your own liking:

```
           O                              O
    NAME OF WINE:          . . . . . . . . . . . . . . . . . .

    DATE STARTED:          . . . . . . . . . . . . . . . . . .

        INGREDIENTS            QUANTITIES
    . . . . . . . . . . . .        . . . . . . . . . . . .
    . . . . . . . . . . . .        . . . . . . . . . . . .
    . . . . . . . . . . . .        . . . . . . . . . . . .
    . . . . . . . . . . . .        . . . . . . . . . . . .
    . . . . . . . . . . . .        . . . . . . . . . . . .

    METHOD:  . . . . . . . . . . . . . . . . . . . . . . . . . . . . . .
    . . . . . . . . . . . . . . . . . . . . . . . . . . . . . . . . . . . . . . . .
    . . . . . . . . . . . . . . . . . . . . . . . . . . . . . . . . . . . . . . . .
    YEAST USED: . . . . . . . . . . . . . . . . . . . . . . . . . . . . . .
```

Prepare the reverse side of the card like this:

O   O

S.G. of must before sugar added: . . . .

S.G. of must after sugar added: . . . .

    Date ferment started: . . . .

    Date ferment ended: . . . .

S.G. at end of fermentation: . . . .

Dates of rackings: Appearance:

    1 . . . .

    2 . . . .

    3 . . . .

Bottled: . . . .

Appreciation: . . . .
. . . .

The card may be filled in as you go along, perhaps on these lines:

O   O

NAME OF WINE: BLACKBERRY

DATE STARTED: 25th August, 1970

    INGREDIENTS   QUANTITIES

    Fresh Blackberries   8 lbs.

    Cold water   6 pts.

    Sugar   2 lbs.

    Cloves   6

    Campden tablet   1

    Nutrient tablet   1

METHOD: Blackberries mashed in water with cloves and Campden tablet. Steeped for 2 days and strained. Sugar, yeast and nutrient stirred in.

YEAST USED: Burgundy.

Reverse side:

O   O

S.G. of must before sugar added: 1·025

S.G. of must after sugar added: 1·100

     Date ferment started: 28th August, 1970

     Date ferment ended: 8th December, 1970

S.G. at end of fermentation: 1·004

Dates of rackings: Appearance:
  1. 15th December, 1970   Clearing
  2. 10th February, 1971   Fine colour
  3. 21st May, 1971   Brilliant

Bottled: 3rd September, 1971.

Appreciation: Good bouquet, fine flavour, dry table wine for special use.

The reason for most of these notes will be obvious to everyone, but one or two explanations may be worth while. The S.G. of the must before the sugar is added is an indication of the quality of the fruit. In other years the gravity may be as low as 10 to 15, and remember that the quality of the fruit does affect the wine.

The S.G. prior to fermentation is of course a predetermined figure depending on the type of wine being made. A port type wine would naturally need additional sugar during fermentation to make a stronger and ultimately a sweeter wine.

Apart from helping a wine to clear, racking helps to mature a wine by admitting a minute quantity of oxygen. This is the period during which a wine develops its flavour and bouquet and so a record of your attentions is essential.

A brief appreciation will be of help in other years to refresh your memory when perhaps the wine has long been consumed.

This easy record will:

1. Provide you with all the information you will need.

2. Hang readily available from the fermentation lock or round the neck of the jar.

3. Being a card it is durable and will not tear easily.

4. It is big enough for normal writing and you don't have to cramp the information into a small space.

5. The card can be stored after use for future reference.

If you are afraid of soiling the card, keep it in one of the small polyethylene bags now about in most homes. A pin through the bag, but not the card, will keep it from falling out.

Alternatively a loose-leaf book with alphabetically indexed guide cards will prove a useful investment, especially if you are interested in doing experimental work. This way sufficient space can easily be provided to keep records as detailed as you wish.

The value of keeping records can hardly be over-emphasized as an aid to improve the standard of your own wine. Learn from your mistakes and repeat your successes.

Chapter 19

BLENDING

INEXPERIENCED WINEMAKERS are often horrified when blending is mentioned to them. It is almost a sacrilege to suggest that a wine they have made is imperfect in any degree, and yet wine is a gift of nature and, therefore, just as fickle. If a dozen people were each to make a given wine from the same ingredients, and if each did exactly the same thing at the same time, it is still highly probable that the result would be a dozen different wines. The difference between some of them might be subtle, but to the knowledgeable palate there would be variations.

One of the reasons why breweries welcome visitors and have no secrets to hide is because they know that no one else can make beer like theirs, because they do not possess the same equipment *in the same building*. It is such subtleties as these that alter the flavour to an extent clearly noticeable to the expert.

Hardly any inexpensive commercial wine you can buy is likely to be made exclusively from only the juice from the grapes of one vineyard in one year. Almost always wines from neighbouring vineyards are blended and sometimes with wines from different years. It is well known that the most important position in a great chateau vineyard, or in a famous shipper's house, is that of the "Tastevin". He is a tremendously skilled artist, for when the chemists have done their best with pasteurization, adjustment of the must, fermentation with a pure yeast culture, racking, filtering and so on, it is the "Tastevin" who says "this wine is not so good as it could be. It is a little dry, a little sweet, lacking body, lacking bite, and so on." It is he who decides what wines to blend together and in what proportion. Upon him rests the responsibility for ensuring that the standard of wine from his firm remains high and that the wine sold is as similar as nature will permit year by year.

And so it is with wine that you make at home. No matter how much use you make of science to aid your production of a perfect wine, something of the artist must also come into play. Your love for the craft of making wine, your judgment of when to do what, your admission that nature has the last word, all have an effect upon the finished wine.

Alas! in spite of every effort, even after using every known scientific aid, some wines do not develop vintage quality nor do they possess the qualities of a sound everyday wine. It is not

114

your fault, they just naturally lack an adequate balance of flavour. Flavour can be affected by variations in temperature, by appearance to the eye, by past experience, by influence of other people's opinion, by tiredness and so on. But these are added differences and the two basic ingredients of flavour consist of smell—or rather aroma, for you smell the aroma—and taste. There are thousands of different smells but oddly enough only four different tastes. These are saltiness, sweetness, bitterness and acidity. In winemaking we need not be concerned with the first, but we are very much concerned with the last three. Of these you are not likely to have much difficulty with sweetness, for if you follow the recommendation to ferment your wines to dryness you can subsequently sweeten to your taste without any trouble.

There remain bitterness and acidity. Both are distinctive when you pause to consider them. Bitterness produces an astringent feeling in the mouth which seems to dry the tongue. Acidity has a sharp sour taste which in excess tends to make you shudder. Sugar is noticed by the taste buds on the upper tip of the tongue, acid on the sides in the front and bitterness on the sides at the back.

A balanced dry wine has acidity and bitterness in such a proportion that neither is pronounced, and if any of your wines are not to your liking, then do blend them together. If you have several wines you wish to blend, first try to achieve balance between wines which are too bitter and those which are not bitter enough. Then do the same for wines which are too sharp and those which are rather flat. When these are in accord, mix together the balanced bitter blend with the balanced acid blend to achieve the perfect whole. In practice it is rarely as complicated as this and the simple blending of two or more wines with differing tastes nearly always results in a happy marriage. If you are in some doubt then first mix just a wineglassful of the two wines and taste. If you find that you need more of one than another try again, varying the proportions as your judgment directs. When you are of the opinion that the wine is now neither acid nor bitter, then mix the bulk together in the proportion that gives you the best result.

Blended wines need storing for some months for the various qualities to harmonize, but invariably you will find greatly improved wines as a result. Often they throw a fresh deposit and achieve new clarity. You need not confine your blending to two wines only. There is no limit to how many you can mix together until you feel that you have found the perfect balance.

Blending can be done as soon as the wine is fermented, but in practice it is usual to leave the wine to mature and see what it makes of itself. If, when it should be ready for drinking, you don't like it, then put it aside until you have another to go with it. It is not a good thing to hurry matters of this sort. No advantage is lost by waiting. On the contrary the wine may improve naturally if left alone. But always leave a blend to harmonize for two or three months before drinking it. During the blending the wine will have absorbed additional oxygen from the air and this needs time to combine with the acids and alcohols for the wine to be at its best.

Most yeasts will ferment a must to an alcoholic strength of about 14% or 15% provided the must contains sufficient nutrients and the fermentation has been carried out correctly. Occasionally a particular yeast will ferment slightly higher and even 18% alcohol may be attained. Generally speaking a higher alcohol content can be achieved by feeding the wine with additional sugar during fermentation as already explained in Chapter 13. But when all this has been done you may decide that a certain wine is such that you would like to increase the alcohol content to about 20% to give the wine that little extra in flavour and longer life. There is no point in adding alcohol solely to increase the potency of a wine. If you want simply to be "knocked out" you will never be a true winemaker, for the true winemaker is concerned far more with the pursuit of quality than of just raw potency. Almost everyone prefers to enjoy a good sound wine for its bouquet and flavour. Some dessert wines, however, especially of the port and sherry type, do benefit from the addition of alcohol, just as do the wines that in fact bear those names. There is little point in adding branded whisky or brandy to your wine, because in these you pay partly for the name and scarcity value. Instead you can use with complete safety and satisfaction either vodka or grain alcohol. Both are distilled from a potato or grain fermentation, have neither flavour nor colour, and will only add alcohol to your wine without disturbing its existing flavour or bouquet.

For a quick calculation 4 fl. ozs. of the strongest vodka increases the alcohol content of a gallon of wine by about 1%. You can find out the precise figures without too much trouble, with the aid of a Pearson Square, but you have to be careful to use the same form of measurement throughout the calculations.

As you know, the alcohol content of a wine is nearly always measured by the volume of alcohol present in a given volume of wine, and we usually refer to our wines as having alcohol content of, for example, 12%. This clearly means that in 100 parts of wine 12 are alcohol and 88 are water, acids, glycerine, etc. We use this method of expressing the content of alcohol because we have simple equipment in the hydrometer and (for dry wines at least) in the vinometer for making the appropriate calculations. In days gone by Excise Officers were less well equipped and they proved whether or not a liquid contained alcohol on which they could levy tax, by pouring some of the liquid over a little pile of gunpowder and applying a spark from a flint. If the powder burnt, then the liquid contained enough alcohol for it to be liable for duty. If the powder was dampened and failed to ignite then the presence of alcohol could not be proved. Custom and tradition survive in England long after their usefulness has finished and accordingly the Customs and Excise Officers still calculate the alcohol content of a wine or whisky in degrees of proof alcohol—but without setting fire to their gunpowder! 100% pure alcohol is reckoned as being 175° Proof. So 100° Proof is therefore equal to only 57·05% alcohol. Since proof values vary from country to country a table of comparisons will be found on page 119.

In England all wines and most spirit are reckoned for duty purposes as so many degrees Proof. For example a whisky advertised as 80° Proof would have an alcohol content of 45·7%. In this manner a wine of say 16% alcohol would be .28° Proof. Your wine is stronger than you think!

Whatever you do, to use a Pearson Square you must work in either Proof or percentage alcohol. You must not mix the measures.

PEARSON SQUARE

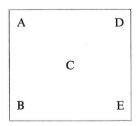

When you wish to fortify a wine, then, draw a little Pearson Square and in the corner marked B write the alcohol content of your wine at present. In the centre marked C write the figure representing the alcohol content you wish to attain. In the corner marked D write the difference between the two figures already entered. Then in the corner marked A write the alcohol content of the vodka you propose to add to your wine and in the corner marked E write the difference between C and A. The proportion D to E is the proportion of vodka you will need to add to your wine to achieve the required increase.

For example—let the present alcohol content of the wine be 15% and the desired figure be 20%. Let us use strong vodka of 80° Proof. First we convert the 80° Proof to percentage alcohol by dividing by 1·75 and this gives a figure of 45·7. Therefore in corner A we write 45·7 and B 15, in C 20, in D 5 (20 – 15) and in E 25·7 (45·7 – 20).

```
A                    D
45·7                 5

          C
          20

B                    E
15                   25·7
```

Therefore we need 5 parts of vodka to 25·7 parts of wine— roughly a fifth. So that to 5 bottles of wine, with an alcohol content of 15%, we should need 1 bottle of strong vodka of 80° Proof to give us a blend of fortified wine of 20% alcohol. A bottle of vodka costs about $6 so the fortification will cost about $1 a bottle as we shall get 6 bottles (5 plus 1).

Here is another method.

If, for instance, you have 11 pts. of really strong wine, say 18%, and you mix with it 1 pt. of brandy at 39·9% (the usual proprietary strength), the percentage of alcohol of the 12 pts. will still be only 19·8%, or 1·8% higher than the unfortified wine.

This can be calculated as follows:

$$\frac{(18 \times 11) + (39·9 \times 1)}{12} = \text{Final percentage of alcohol}$$

$$\frac{198 + 39·9}{12} = \frac{237·9}{12} = 19·8\%$$

Those who are likely to consider fortifying their wines may also wish to experiment with liqueur flavours provided by extracts, the best known of which come from the T. Noirot Laboratories. A very wide range of 30 or 40 different flavours is usually available at the moderate cost of from 30¢ to 75¢ a little bottle, sufficient to flavour one bottle of liqueur. A few of the extracts can be used with a bottle of sweet or dry wine. These include red and golden aperitifs and French and Italian vermouths. You simply add the extract to the wine, with an ounce or two of additional sugar if needed, shake it up and store it for a month or two. They are effective if used with a good sound wine which is perhaps lacking in flavour and bouquet.

The liqueurs proper have to be added to sugar, water and spirit in the form of either brandy, vodka, rum, whisky or gin. First pour 10 oz. of hot water onto at least 10 ozs. and preferably 12 ozs. of granulated sugar. Stir thoroughly till the sugar is dissolved and the water has lost sufficient of its heat not to crack a 26-oz· wine bottle when it is poured in. Then add the chosen extract and fill up with alcohol, cork tightly, give the bottle a good shake and store for two months. Certain flavours mix better with given alcohols than others, and the Noirot Laboratories recommend as follows:

With Whisky use: Reverendine, Cream of Apricot, Cream of Mirabelle, Cherry Brandy; Cream of Cacao, Curacao, Yellow and Green Convent, Mandarine, Peach and Prunelle.

With Gin use: Cream of Green or White Mint, Yellow or Green Convent, Curacao, Danzig, Kummel and Anisette.

With Brandy or Rum use: Cream of Apricot, Cream of Green Mint, Moka, Cream of Mirabelle, Cream of Cacao, Cherry Brandy, Yellow or Green Convent, Peach, Prunelle, Curacao and Orange.

PROOF COMPARISON TABLE

% Alcohol by Volume	British Degrees of Proof	Canadian Proof	U.S. Proof
100	175	75 Over Proof	200
86	150	50 O.P.	172
71·5	125	25 O.P.	143
57·1	100	Proof	114
50	87	13 Under Proof	100
43	75	25 U.P.	86
40	70	30 U.P.	80
29	50	50 U.P.	58
14	25	75 U.P.	28
0	0	100 U.P.	0

Chapter 20

AILMENTS OF WINE

W HOLE BOOKS have been devoted to the subject of this chapter. The thought is frightening until you think of the enormous number of books written on human ailments and then recall that the majority of people keep remarkably well most of the time. The secret of health for humans is mainly good living and the present medical emphasis is on disease prevention rather than cure. It is the same with wine. The emphasis is on prevention rather than cure.

Make sure that *all* your equipment is perfectly clean *all* the time.

Make sure that the must is free from harmful bacteria before fermentation is started.

Always use a fermentation trap.

Make sure that your must has sufficient acidity, tannin and nutrient and do use a good yeast.

Don't overboil and don't be afraid to use a Campden tablet.

If you make a strong healthy wine and store it in chemically clean containers you will never need to refer to this chapter. Keep in the forefront of your mind that wonderfully applicable adage: "Prevention is better than cure".

If, like Homer, you nod once in a while then perhaps these notes will help you.

The most common cause of wine spoilage is probably acetification. The vinegar bacillus, mycoderma aceti, floats invisibly in the air, with yeast cells and other micro-organisms. It settles on your hands, fruit and equipment. It is also carried by the tiny fruit fly which swarms about damaged fruit. At times the mycoderma aceti cells are actually deposited *in* those plums whose skins have been penetrated by wasps, for example, or have been damaged in handling. The cells rapidly multiply and could cause failure in wine made from that fruit unless properly treated beforehand.

Although prevention of acetification is simple, cure is almost impossible and, frankly, not worth the trouble. Prevent acetification, them, by the following means:

1. Sterilize your equipment and must with boiling water or with sulphite.
2. Always use a fermentation trap with one-eighth of a Campden tablet in the water in the trap, or with glycerine instead of this sulphite. Alternatively use plain water in

the bend and lightly plug the outlet with cotton wool to keep out the vinegar fly.

3. Always keep your containers full and keep out the air.

If the cork in a bottle of wine is old, porous or dry, so that the fit is not perfect, another microbe known as mycoderma vini may penetrate and settle on the surface of the wine, then multiplying and forming a whitish film known as "flowers of wine". This little germ slowly breaks down the alcohol in the wine into carbon dioxide and water and consequently the wine tastes flat and lifeless. Both mycoderma aceti and mycoderma vini need plenty of air in which to grow and this is the obvious clue to the prevention of damage from these sources. Furthermore both of these micro-organisms are unable to grow in wine containing more than 10% alcohol. We repeat—always keep your must and wine in containers which *exclude* the air.

Acetification of wine can be noticed in an instant by the unmistakable vinegary smell and taste. The mycoderma vini forms a film on the top of a still wine to which the air has access, and can be seen clearly.

The next ailment to be discussed is also easy to spot. If a wine appears to be thicker than you would expect when you pour it from the bottle, then it has been attacked by bacteria, short and rod-like, which grow together in long chains giving a slimy effect to the wine. It usually occurs in young wines during *storage* and can be cured by adding two Campden tablets to the gallon of wine and by stirring it vigorously to break up the chains. The wine should be then filtered or fined, rebottled and treated as normal. The wine is not harmed.

If, when you hold your wine to the light and agitate it gently, you see a silky cloud, then your wine has been attacked by another bacteria, this time shaped like a long rod. It causes excess bitterness and off flavours sometimes described as "mousey". It is known as the "Tourne disease" in places and as the "bitter disease" in others. The cure again lies with Campden tablets, stirring and filtering. The cause is often residual sugar and this ailment does not often occur in strong dry wines.

From time to time you may hear of a disease known as "casse" or "break" to give it an English translation. In appearance a wine ailing from "casse" has a coloured haziness or even cloudy appearance. The cause this time is not bacterial but metal poisoning. If iron or copper or tin is allowed to come into contact with the must or wine for any length of time, some metal will be dissolved by the acids in the liquor. Even in a proportion of 3 parts of metal in a million parts of wine, cloudiness is caused; but sometimes the concentration is as high as

25 parts in a million. The addition of some citric acid will prevent the precipitation (i.e. will stop it from getting worse), but will not remove the metallic salts causing the haze. It is recommended that the wine be aerated by stirring, some tannin be added (a tablespoonful of cold strong tea, to the gallon of wine) and the wine subsequently fined. When the precipitate has settled, rack the wine and add 1% or 2% citric acid to prevent further trouble. It can clearly be seen, once more, that prevention of "casse" by not using metal containers is very much easier than its cure.

Sometimes when a wine develops a haze this may be due to undissolved pectin. This is probable if the fruit has been boiled and no Pectolase added subsequently. A simple check can be made by mixing 3 or 4 parts of methyl alcohol with 1 part of wine. The indication for pectin haze is the appearance in the mixture of jelly-like clots or strings. Happily the cure is not difficult. From 1 gal. of wine remove ½ pt. and add ½ oz. of Pectolase. Stir the mixture occasionnally or shake it in a bottle and keep it in a warm temperature, 70°–80° F., for up to 4 hrs. Strain the liquid through a nylon sieve and add it to the bulk of the wine which should be kept in a warm room, 60°–70° F., for several days. The pectin haze should precipitate and settle so that the clear wine can be racked into a fresh container, but if the haze does not settle out quickly enough it can now be removed effectively with the aid of finings.

In wines made from cereals and sometimes apples, minute particles of starch occasionally produce a haze. If there is no reaction from the methyl alcohol test add a few drops of iodine. If the solution turns blue then your wine has a starch haze. The remedy for this is the use of Amylozyme 100. For a gallon of wine, ½ oz. of Amylozyme 100 is mixed with 2 to 3 ozs. of water and left for 2 hrs., stirring (or shaking if in a bottle) at intervals. While this is going on put the wine into a preserving pan and heat to 170° F. and hold this for 20 mins. Cool the wine to 110° F. and stir in the diluted Amylozyme 100. In about 1 hr. the reaction will be complete and the temperature of the wine should again be raised to 170° F. and held for 10 mins. After cooling the haze will settle out and the wine should be racked.

When a wine remains cloudy and reacts to none of the tests mentioned, resource must be had to fining—always the last remedy. More than the clouding may be removed with the finings and the wine left without sufficient body. Don't fine a wine unless you have to. If you do, it is worth while buying some Serena wine finings specially prepared for the purpose.

Full instructions accompany the bottle and won't be discussed here. Gelatin can be used, especially in conjunction with tannin, but tests have to be made to ascertain the correct amounts to use and you really need a laboratory to do so. Isinglass is cheap, but by no means easy to use. Although full instructions are given in the packet, the result rarely is what one expects. The secret is to grind up the fine straw-like fibres into a powder and to dissolve them in a little tartaric acid and a small quantity of wine. The solution is more effective if left overnight so that the finings can be mixed into the bulk of the wine as a finely beaten up jelly and not as crumbs of isinglass. Although the wine may clear in a few days it sometimes takes weeks to do so, but is then brilliantly clear.

Asbestos pulp is probably the best and simplest agent to use for filtering. A handful of pulp is usually sufficient to remove the solids from several gallons of wine. The pulp looks rather like kapok and is prepared by placing it in a basin, pouring a small quantity of wine over it and then "whipping" it up with a fork just as you would beat up an egg. Keep on beating till the pulp is as frothy as possible, taking perhaps 10 minutes to do so. Now place a plug of cotton wool in the bottom of a very large funnel and pour in the frothy asbestos pulp. Place a saucer over the pulp, reaching to the sides of the funnel. When the wine is poured in, it falls onto the saucer and gently over-flows onto the pulp but does not stir it up or disturb it. Fill the funnel to the brim and cover with a cloth to keep out the dust and germs. The first wineglassful of wine that comes through the pulp should be returned for further filtering, but after that the wine dripping through will be found clear and bright.

Two teaspoonfuls of milk to the gallon of wine are sometimes effective. The acidity in the wine clots the milk and as these clots settle they take down the offending insoluble particles in the wine.

Generally then, prevent ailments by absolute cleanliness, ex-clude the air from must and wine, ferment to dryness by using a good yeast aided by an adequate nutrient in an acid must with a sufficiency of tannin and *not too much sugar*.

Chapter 21

THE ART OF APPRECIATION

ALTHOUGH THERE is undoubtedly very great pleasure in making wine at home, the greatest pleasure of all is surely in the appreciation of the good wine that you drink. Even in appreciation, however, there is a technique which enables you to increase your satisfaction. Usually this technique is applied only by connoisseurs, but if you are making and drinking wine regularly you will quickly develop an experience and knowledge of wines both of your own and commercial wines.

Surprisingly perhaps, the amateur winemaker is often a buyer of the better types of foreign wines. At "Annual Dinners" and on similar occasions you will find that your knowledge of wine is a great help in choosing a suitable wine to accompany your meal. Some information on the technique of appreciation, then, will add to your pleasure on all occasions. You will seek out the attributes and judge a wine on its quality and not on its name.

Perhaps the first thing to learn is how to hold a glass of wine. You might think that there can be two ways of doing such a simple thing and that it is obviously best to hold the glass by the stem and the bowl. When you are simply drinking wine, then this is certainly the normal way, but when you are appreciating a wine there is a better way.

The next time you are offered a glass take it by the base with your thumb on the top and your forefinger and middle finger beneath as you would a plate. The glass can be held quite firmly and you will find this is a much more convenient grip when you are swirling the wine in the glass to release the volatile esters. Before swirling the wine, however, examine it, scrutinize the colour, the clarity, the brilliance, the texture. Does the colour appeal or does it possess some doubtful shade or sheen? Is the wine perfectly clear and free from haze of any kind? Does it shine with a true brilliance when you hold it up to the light? Has it such a splendid rich colouring that you can say that it has a magnificent "robe"? Look for all these things in your own wines that you have made yourself. Elderberry wine is one that should certainly have a "robe" when examined in front of a lighted candle or unshaded electric light bulb.

And then look at the texture. Does it appear thin or thick or exactly right for a wine of its type? Give it an exploratory swirl and have a look at the wine as it slides down the side of the glass. Can you see the folds in the wine? Does the sight of the wine in general provide a feast for your eyes? You should enjoy the wine with your eyes first of all.

Having spent a few moments in visual enjoyment and anticipation, the time has come to use your nose and to satisfy your sense of smell. Take a gentle whiff at first, merely passing the glass from side to side under your nostrils. Can you detect the perfume of the fruits or flowers concerned? Does it smell appetizing?

All the chemical reactions between acids, alcohols and aldehydes which have gone on in the bottle over the months and years were destined for this moment. Do not let it pass by unnoticed. Make the most of it and savour the wine to the utmost. Take several good substantial sniffs—nothing delicate and fancy, but really full-blooded and robust. Let your nose enjoy itself for a change.

By now several minutes may have passed since you accepted the glass of wine and you have not yet tasted it. But your eyes and nose have feasted and your mouth is no doubt watering as it waits its turn. The moment is not far off. Have one last look and then take, not a sip, but a mouthful. Be ready to take notice of the "greeting" the wine gives you, the very first taste upon your tongue. Roll the wine around your mouth so that it reaches every taste bud and you can absorb the flavour to the full. Then be prepared as you swallow for the "farewell"— that is the taste as the wine passes over the palate on its journey to your stomach. Pause now to appreciate the after taste as the wine goes down.

Was the wine dry, medium, sweet or syrupy? What about the flavour? Was it round and smooth or were there some rough elements? Did the wine have plenty of body or was it thin? Was the tannin content about right, providing good "bite", or was it flabby? Acid, as you know, is an important element, but it must not intrude. Did the wine taste sharp, denoting too much acid, or did you find it mellow enough? And how about age? Did you think the wine was rather "young" yet, hadn't reached maturity, or calamity! was it mordant and past its best?

Stop for a moment more to co-ordinate in your mind the relative pleasures enjoyed by your eyes, your nose and our tongue. Consider your opinion before you express your pleasure in the spoken word.

Some time at home try to compare one of your wines with another. Jot down the characteristics mentioned above on a sheet of paper and award yourself marks for each wine according to their relative merits. Try to seek out each point individually. It is like listening to an orchestra. You can hear all of the instruments separately. So, too, with wine; you can enjoy all the qualities together in a harmonious whole or you can separate them and concentrate on each one for a moment or two. This way you will find that you can enjoy your wine to the full and derive a great deal more satisfaction from your endeavours.

Chapter 22

SERVING YOUR WINE

EVERY ASPECT of winemaking is important. The preparation of the must determines the type of wine, the fermentation can have great influence on its quality, good cellar-craft will improve the wine anyway, but at the end of it all an enormous amount depends on the way you serve your wine. Hurriedly taken from your store, perhaps disturbing the sediment, served without regard for cooling or room temperature and then drunk from a tumbler on an empty stomach—that would be enough to put anyone off wine for life!

Throughout recorded history poets have praised wine with the most apt phrases and the choicest rhymes. For them an occasion for drinking wine was also one for ceremony and in spite of their lack of scientific knowledge it must be obvious that, sometimes at least, winemakers must have excelled themselves and stimulated the muse with a superb potion. It is well to recall something of these sentiments when you serve your own wine.

The late Maurice Healy—one of the greatest connoisseurs of recent years—said, in effect, that you should only serve your best wine to your most discriminating friends and then only on high occasions. There were other wines for other friends and other occasions, and what was the use of wasting your best wine on someone who could not appreciate it to the full? There are times when every amateur winemaker produces a really tip-top wine and he rarely has more than one gallon, just six bottles of it. Enjoy these wines for yourself, sharing your jubilation with none but your very best friends. But enjoy them to the full by serving them to perfection—even for yourself.

Not every wine you make will satisfy your standards, and many experienced winemakers are happy if out of ten different wines, three are excellent, five are quite good and only two are below par. These two perhaps—and indeed, some of the five too—can be blended and so improved, but more about blending elsewhere.

Wine can safely and beneficially be served in moderation to almost everyone, young and old, well and not so well.

Wine has long had a reputation for therapeutic benefits and in country districts different wines were regarded as specific for certain ailments, for example, celery wine was said to give great relief to those suffering from rheumatism. In every country and in all ages of recorded history, wine has had a special place in medicine. Medical research has shown that the alcohol and any residual unfermented sugar is readily assimilable as a source of energy. The mineral elements, particularly potassium, are of positive value in nutrition and in the digestive system. Many wines, especially those in which Campden tablets have not been used, are particularly rich in Vitamin B1. Unfortunately this vitamin is destroyed by the sulphur dioxide released into the wine by Campden tablets.

A glass of wine is often prescribed by doctors as an appetizer and is therefore of great help to those recovering from illness. Taken in moderation, wine stimulates all the gastric juices, creates desire for food and assists in its digestion. In moderation again, it has a beneficial effect on the heart, liver and kidneys, relaxes the nervous system and eases tension. It has no ill effect on the lungs and may be taken with benefit by those recovering from pulmonary ailments. Alcohol in any form, however, should be avoided by those suffering from acute pneumonia.

All wines are of help and comfort to the aged. Dessert wines at bedtime help them to relax and assist them to sleep naturally. Dry wines are of benefit to those who suffer from diabetes. Sweet wines should obviously be avoided by them but dry wines which are free from sugar encourage a feeling of well-being in diabetics and the alcohol can be assimilated safely.

Some medicines are in fact mixed with wine, since certain substances are soluble in a solution of 12%–20% alcohol which are not soluble in water.

Medical research has clearly shown that almost everyone can benefit from the moderate use of wines, but the word moderate is most important. Taken in excess over a long period harm will certainly be caused. Always enjoy your wine in moderation.

When you feel that a certain wine is ready for drinking, test its brilliance against the light, handling the bottle carefully in case of any deposit. Remove the capsule and insert a corkscrew to the limit. Use either a corkscrew with a wide screw—the fine ones tend to pull through a really tight-fitting cork—or one of the cork extractors, which insert a blade down either side of the cork. When you have a firm grip of the cork pull strongly and steadily, avoiding any jerking or rebound of the bottle. The inside neck and mouth of the bottle should be wiped with a clean cloth before you pour out half a glassful. If it is a red wine, warm it a little in the bowl of your hand, smelling the bouquet from time to time before tasting it. If it is a white wine, it may be tasted straight from storage, since 50°–55° F. (10–13° C.) will be cool enough for this purpose. If you have fermented your wine in the manner recommended, your wine will be dry, perhaps too dry for your palate. The wine can easily be sweetened by mixing a little of the wine with say 1 oz. (30 grams) of sugar, and when it is dissolved, adding it to the rest. If 1 oz. is not enough, then add another ½ oz. or so until you think it just right. Such sweetening is best done in a decanter or jug and not in the bottle itself. The wine should first be decanted from any sediment which may have accumulated.

It is most important to serve your wine absolutely brilliant and quite free from haze of any kind. Unquestionably, too, wine looks its best in a plain glass decanter. It is so much more elegant to have a polished decanter upon your table than a bottle, however beautifully labelled. Furthermore, when wine is poured into a decanter it is naturally aerated and this not only enables some dissolved carbon dioxide to escape, but also converts certain of the volatile acids and alcohols into esters, the fragrant aroma of which you will be able to smell with great pleasure. Again, if the wine is red the larger surface exposed to the air will absorb the temperature of the room more quickly. If left *too* long in a decanter, however, the oxidation will proceed to the state of decomposition and your wine will grow flat and lifeless. There is every good reason for serving your wine in a decanter and none at all for serving it from the bottle.

Before you actually serve, however, do make sure that your wine is at the right temperature. Wines rich in body and colour and strong in alcohol nearly always benefit enormously by allowing them to breathe and warm up in the room in which they are to be served. Such wines include nearly all the red, like blackberry and elderberry, and some of the rich golden wines such as parsnip, which may be served as a dessert wine. The ideal temperature is in the region of 65°–70° F. (17—21° C.). On the other hand white wines and pale pink wines dry and light in body are better cooled before serving. The bottle or the decanter of wine may be stood in the refrigerator for an hour or the decanter may be stood in a glass dish and surrounded with ice chips to achieve a temperature of 40°–50° F. (5–10° C.). Ice should never be added to the wine since it will dilute the wine with water as it melts.

If you propose to serve several wines with a meal—and this has much to commend it—it is a useful rule always to serve your dry and delicate-flavoured wines before your sweeter or stronger ones. Once you have tasted a sweet wine your palate will be spoiled for a dry. Your choice will be dependent upon what you have available and the food you propose to eat with it. The rule of the "red wine with red meat, and white wine for white meat and fish" is a sound general guide so long as it doesn't preclude your enjoying any particular wine with any food you happen to choose if you like it so. The diversity of human nature is such that only you can decide what wine you enjoy best with any chosen food. So if you want to drink an excellent apple wine with roast beef then by all means do so.

When wines are served other than with a meal it is not wise to drink too heavily. Wines made at home are often very potent, and unless you know that you can drink a bottle of port wine without turning a hair, then don't attempt to drink the same quantity of your own wine unaccompanied. Dry wines and aperitifs may be served alone before a meal, but dessert wines, whether they be golden or ruby, are best accompanied by a shortbread or piece of fruit cake for those with a sweet tooth and by savoury biscuits for others. Almost any wine goes well with almost any cheese, except perhaps the strong-flavoured gorgonzola types.

The glasses in which you serve your wine should be chosen with as much care as you can afford. Remember that your eyes and nose have their part to play as well as your mouth, when you are drinking wine. Avoid fussy or painted glasses which are distracting. Choose thin colourless glasses that are at once pleasing to the eye, and sufficiently tulip-shaped to enable the aroma to collect and not be dissipated. For all purposes a stemmed glass is preferable. It enables you to see the wine to its best advantage and, by handling the base, no fingermarks are made upon the bowl to impair your view. A 5-oz. goblet is most suitable for table wines and illustrations are given for other varieties. Before using them, glasses should be polished with a clean dry linen cloth that does not leave little hairs behind. Pour the wine into the glass slowly and carefully so as not to slop any on the outside of the glass and *never* fill the glass full, but only between a half and two-thirds. This leaves space for the esters to collect on the surface of the wine so that you can readily savour them. It also leaves space for you to swirl the wine around by gently revolving the glass to encourage the further formation of esters.

Table wines should not be too strong in alcoholic content and you should bear this in mind when preparing your must. An alcoholic content from 10% to 12% by volume is quite enough for table wine. Dessert wines can be from 12% to 17% and even higher if you care to fortify them. It is unlikely that you will often get a naturally stronger wine, however, but this is plenty for enjoyment, if the other characteristics of bouquet, flavour and body are satisfactory.

Liqueurs, of course, are fortified wines and are served after a meal and in small glasses, for they are strong and sweet, often almost cloying.

Knowing that you have made the wine yourself, your guests will certainly appreciate a few words from you about each wine as you serve it. You could perhaps mention something about the basic ingredients, such as parsnips or elderberry, whether you used any particular yeast, when the wine was made and maybe some comment about how long it took to ferment or to clear, whether it is dry, medium or sweet. Or you can ask them to tell you what type of wine they think it is and then you can tell them the answers.

The point is very well worth bearing in mind and there is no doubt that it will add much to your guests' enjoyment of your wine.

At some time or another you should certainly experiment with cooking with wine and there are many inexpensive books to help you with recipes. In general wines made at home may be used just as freely as commercial wines. Indeed recipes recommending commercial wines often specify "cooking sherry" or "cheap red wine" and the like. At home, you will have wines superior to these for cooking purposes and your results will be that much better. You need not be afraid that the children will become intoxicated, because the alcohol comes off during cooking. Where there are no children to be considered you may add your wine freely to trifles or wine jellies, to gravy just before serving, to casseroles and to roasting poultry; fish baked in wine is superb and apples stewed in white wine are a luxury.

Strong red wines are excellent when mulled. Heat the wine to a temperature of about 160°F. (71°C.) in a saucepan with some sugar lumps previously rubbed on a lemon skin, add a few cloves, a little root ginger and a little grated nutmeg and such other spices as you like, always too little rather than too much. Some rum may also be added and, with advantage, brandy.

Serve the hot punch in glasses containing a silver spoon to prevent the heat from cracking the glasses. This is an excellent drink with which to greet guests on a cold night, or better still to give them before they set off home in the snow. It should, of course, not be served instead of an aperitif before a full meal, because the strong flavours and high alcohol content would spoil the palate for other wines.

The following menu may be found a useful guide in serving your wines:

As an aperitif: Any white wine flavoured with an aperitif extract, or a dry fruit wine such as orange.

With soup or fish: A dry mead or white wine, e.g. apple.

With roast beef, lamb or turkey: A medium red wine, e.g. plum or blackberry.

With fruit dessert or Christmas pudding: Any white wine, full, sweet and strong.

Cheese: A red wine of character, e.g. elderberry.

Coffee and petits fours: Cherry brandy or other liqueur.

This does not claim to be more than a rough guide, since any of the wines mentioned can be made sweet or dry according to the quantity of sugar used in the fermentation. Furthermore, if you have used specific yeast types in your fermentation, your wines will closely resemble the wine from which the yeast was obtained. Nevertheless, it is an indication of what can be achieved and an idea of the order in which your wines should be served. It does not preclude individual varaitions to suit your taste.

But do not get the impression that wine should be reserved solely for the high occasion and the exalted guest. An appropriate wine served with casseroled steak or meat pie, etc., etc., with only the family at table can enhance the meal and give health and enjoyment to the participants — but do serve the wine at the right temperature from a decanter into suitable glasses even when no one is looking.

Chapter 23

MEAD

A s STATED earlier, there is evidence to suggest that mead is the oldest known fermented drink. Possibly some thirsty caveman stumbled across a beehive in the hollow of a fallen tree after a storm. Maybe the honey had trickled into the water and the wild yeasts had rapidly fermented it slightly. The liquid would have tasted pleasingly different to someone living on a dull diet of meat and berries. Before long, no doubt, he mastered the art of mixing honey, or whatever he called it, with water and allowing it to stand until by his standards it turned into a very worthwhile drink.

Whatever the true story is, there is no doubt that man has been making mead for many thousands of years. After it was found that beeswax made excellent candles, innumerable hives would be kept by religious houses and all those who could afford to do so. While sugar was still a great luxury in the sixteenth, seventeenth and eighteenth centuries, honey was used for sweetening as well. The bee population must have been enormous compared with today.

But with the coming of oil lamps and cheaper sugar the need for honey declined and the art of making mead fell into disuse.

In more recent years, amateur bee-keepers no doubt sometimes, if not often, made mead from old recipes handed down, but the price of English honey prevented many from experimenting with this ancient, satisfying and wholly delightful drink. Happily, excellent honey is now imported, usually in 7-lb. packs and at a cost of about 1s. 9d. per lb. Different varieties can be bought, such as orange blossom honey from California or Spain and clover honey from New Zealand. While both liquid and crystal honey can be used, the crystal tends to have a higher sugar content and therefore the same amount of honey ferments to a higher degree than a given quantity of liquid honey. If you have your own bees the comb washings can also be used but the liquid will need concentrating to remove some of the water, and increase the proportion of sugar.

A particular advantage of making mead is that it can be made at any time of the year. If you feel so inclined, for example, you can make a brew every month to keep up a regular supply. Furthermore, you can make it just whenever it is convenient to *you* instead of when the ripeness of fruit demands attention. And again from the one basic ingredient you can make a full range of different wines by varying the proportion of honey and water, adding spices or fruit juces and fermenting with different yeasts.

True mead is the product of the fermentation of honey and water without any other addition except the nutrients to strengthen the yeast. When additions of spices, such as ginger, cloves, mace and cinnamon, are made the wine is called metheglin. When fruit juices are added the wine is called melomel. There is some doubt as to whether sack mead is a strong sweet wine of the Madeira type of whether "sack" is a corruption of "sec" meaning dry. The older recipes would appear to make a dry wine, but nowadays a sack mead is usually of an alcohol content of 14% to 15% and slightly sweet into the bargain. Honey may also be used instead of sugar in wine recipes and some are quite successful. Experienced mead makers, however, are generally of the opinion today that the result is neither one thing nor the other. A thousand years ago, on the other hand, there were innumerable variations of alcoholic drinks using honey as a main ingredient. A famous drink of the well-to-do was known as pyment or piment. This was a mixture of grape juice (sometimes already fermented) and honey. Very often, spices were added and the brew was then called "hippocras". This had a great many variations with names associated with the Church such as Pope, Cardinal and Bishop. Sometimes the brew was served hot and one can well imagine such a drink being used successfully in place of the central heating of modern civilization!

Natural honey lacks certain ingredients necessary to a good wine, and contains many impurities. It is, therefore, necessary to simmer the honey and water together, skimming off the impurities as they arise until the liquid is clear. A preserving kettle or large saucepan may be used, and if your vessel isn't large enough to contain both honey and water, use only some of the water and add the remainder later. But use at least as much water as honey or else foaming will be troublesome to control. To prevent the honey burning to the bottom of the kettle, heat the water first and stir in the honey, dissolving it before it touches the bottom. At this stage also include the nutrient salts.

After simmering, the must should be strained through a fine-meshed cloth such as nylon and then cooled as quickly as possible, keeping it carefully covered meanwhile. The tannin can now be added in the form of grape tannin, according to the supplier's instructions, or simply by a tablespoonful of cold strong tea. The maximum quantity of acids and nutrients necessary for 1 Imperial gal. of water added to 3½ lbs. of honey is as follows:

Tartaric acid	80 grains	(5 grams)
Ammonium sulphate	60 grains	(4 g.)
Magnesium sulphate	8 grains	(½ g.)
Citric acid	55 grains	(3½ g.)
Potassium phosphate	30 grains	(2 g.)
Common salt	30 grains	(2 g.)

Use less or more in proportion. Most druggists will make this up for a matter of pennies. It should be noted that the compound is hygroscopic and will absorb moisture from the air, making it into a rather sticky paste. Accordingly it is best to keep it in an airtight container until required for use. Any type of yeast will ferment mead satisfactorily, but the different yeasts will of course give different flavours. There is a special mead yeast known as Maury which can be obtained in culture or tablet form, but almost any wine yeast can be used with success; baker's yeast *can* be used, but may affect the rather delicate flavour. Brewer's yeast may also be used, especially if you are making honey beer with hops.

Yeast is best added to a mead must as it is to a wine must, in the form of a starter, so that the main fermentation can get away quickly. The vigorous fermentation will last 2 or 3 weeks, after which a slower fermentation will continue until the mead is dry or the yeast has reached its maximum alcohol tolerance. With a sweet mead this may take up to 2 years. After 6 weeks it is best to rack the mead into a clean and dry vessel. Check the specific gravity if you have a hydrometer and remember that it is dangerous to cork tightly until the reading is 1·005 or lower. If the reading is higher replace the fermentation trap and leave the jar in a temperature around 70° F. (21° C.). When fermenting during the winter it is not always easy to maintain this temperature and it is a great advantage to have a fermentation cupboard or a thermostatically controlled immersion heater to help you.

If mead is racked occasionally and left long enough it will fall bright and may then be racked into bottles, corked, sealed and stored and served just like any other wine. If it doesn't clear naturally it may be fined like other wines. Lighter meads of lower alcoholic content mature more quickly than stronger sweeter meads, but if mead is drunk young the faint taste of honey remains. When it is adequately matured this distinctive flavour, which some people dislike, disappears and is replaced by one more mellow.

Honey consists of dextrose and laevulose sugars, both entirely fermentable by wine yeasts, and innumerable traces of other elements. For example, a bottle of mead made from a flower honey will consist of the nectar of something like 30,000 flowers. 2 lbs. of honey in an Imperial gallon of water gives a specific gravity of 1·060. So also does 1 Kg. honey in 5 litres of water.

1½ Kg. or 3 lbs. gives 1·090

2   Kg. or 4 lbs. gives 1·120

2½ Kg. or 5 lbs. gives 1·150

4 lbs. of honey *to* a gallon of water is equal to 3 lbs. of honey *in* a gallon.

The following recipes are but guides and may be varied to suit your own tastes or circumstances.

DRY MEAD

	Imperial	U.S.	Metric
Honey	3-3½ lb.	2½-3 lb.	1½-1¾ kilo.
Water	1 gallon	1 gallon	5 litres

Nutrient salts and yeast.

After simmering and cooling S.G. is likely to be about 1·100. Cool, add yeast and ferment right out before racking.

SWEET MEAD

	Imperial	U.S.	Metric
Honey	4-4½ lb.	3½-3¾ lb.	2-2¼ kilo.
Water	1 gallon	1 gallon	5 litres

Nutrient salts, yeast.

Simmer as prescribed and cool· Subsequent S.G. about 1·120· Ferment as usual.

SACK MEAD

	Imperial	U.S.	Metric
Honey	5-5½ lb.	4¼-4¾ lb.	2½-2¾ kilo.
Water	1 gallon	1 gallon	5 litres

Nutrient salts and yeast.

N.B· It is recommended that you start with 4–4½ lbs. of honey per Imperial gallon, as for a sweet mead, and stir in the other 1 lb. of honey when the first tumultuous fermentation subsides· Aerate the must to invigorate the yeast when you add the honey. Ferment in the warm for as long as possible and do not rack till fermentation is quite finished.

The lower weight in the recipes is for crystalline honey and the higher for liquid honey. Pale honeys are generally of a more delicate flavour. In dark honeys the flavour is more pronounced and it is therefore recommended for metheglins, etc. The specific gravity will depend on the amount of sugar and water already in the honey, but the figure can be adjusted by the amount of water you add. The figures given here are therefore guides only.

By using a gallon of water to the amount of honey, there will be a small quantity of must left over after simmering, and this may be used for topping up·

METHEGLIN

	Imperial	U.S.	Metric
Dark Honey	4½ lb.	3¾ lb·	2¼ kilo.
Water	1 gallon	1 gallon	5 litres
Mace, cloves, cinnamon, bruised ginger	1 oz. ea.	1 oz. ea.	30 g. each

Thin rind of 1 lemon and 1 orange.
Nutrient salts and yeast.

Simmer together, strain off and cool before fermenting. Needs long maturation.

MELOMEL

	Imperial	U.S.	Metric
Honey	3½ lb.	3 lb.	1¾ kilo.
Mixed summer fruits: redcurrants, raspberries, a few blackcurrants, gooseberries, black cherries, as available	4 lb.	3½ lb.	2 kilo.
Water	1 gallon	1 gallon	5 litres

Nutrient and all-purpose yeast.

Pour boiling water over fruit, leave overnight, mash next day and leave another 24 hrs· Strain, add the honey and nutrient salts and simmer as with other meads. Cool, add the yeast starter and ferment as usual. Rack and store for 2 years.

HONEY BEER

	Imperial	U.S.	Metric
Honey	1½ lb.	1¼ lb.	¾ kilo.
Water	1 gallon	1 gallon	5 litres
Hops	1 oz.	1 oz.	30 grams

A little yeast nutrient

Simmer together for 1 hr. Strain, cool and ferment rapidly by using previously prepared starter of brewer's yeast. After 2 weeks rack into screw-top bottles. Ready in 2 or 3 weeks.

Variations of these basic recipes may be made by yourself *ad infinitum*.

Chapter 24

BEER

IN CHAPTER I reference was made to the fact that winemaking was well known to the ancient Egyptian civilization, and it seems clear on the evidence available that they also knew how to make ale and did in fact do so. It probably had little similarity with the best bottled beer that you can buy today, but nevertheless it was fermented from a solution of malt and flavoured with wild herbs. And this was 3,000 years before Christ! Ale was well known to the ancient Hebrews and the word Schekar used by Moses probably referred to an intoxicating drink prepared from barley. Hops were also well known, and there is a Rabbinical tradition that the Jews were free from leprosy during the captivity in Babylon by reason of their drinking Schekar made bitter with hops. The Greek word for Schekar was Sicera from which we get our English word cider, but it seems unlikely on the face of it that hops would be used in cider which has plenty of flavour compared with "barley wine" which lacks "bite".

Among the Gauls, Germans, Scandinavians, Celts and Saxons ale became a national beverage. The word "ale" appears to be of Scandinavian origin, whilst the word "beer" seems to spring from the Teutonic language. The words ale and beer are now used indiscriminately, though for centuries ale referred to the unhopped brew and beer to that containing hops.

Ale was made in England before the Romans landed, for it was they who introduced the hop as the most suitable flavouring and preservative, yet for the next 1,500 years other flavourings were used—notably the nettle—and it was not until the fifteenth century that the use of hops became general. During the Hundred Years War English soldiers got to like the hopped "bière" of Flandęrs, and when they returned home they demanded hopped ale which they called beer.

Athanaeus tells us that at the end of the second century A.D. ale was the regular drink of the poorer classes in England. By the fifth century, however, it had crept up the social scale and was competing with mead as the drink of the wealthy. Among the Danes and Anglo-Saxons ale was certainly the favourite beverage and its virtues are celebrated in many of their ancient poems. They used the long horns of their cattle as containers from which to drink, and a favourite contest was to empty a horn in one go. This was no mean feat since the horn could contain a quart of beer and led to the phrase "a yard of ale".

After the Norman Conquest and the tremendous impetus then given to English civilization, brewing steadily became something of an industry. Most Abbeys had their own breweries, which supplied the needs of immediate neighbours, but breweries supplying the needs of others were also at work. In the reign of Henry IV a guild known as the "Mistery of Free Brewers" was in existence in London. A century and a half later, 1437 to be exact, Henry VI granted a charter to the Worshipful Company of Brewers, giving them power to control "the mistery and processes connected with brewing any kind of malt liquor in the City and its suburbs for ever". And it still does.

By the middle ages, then, beer had become the general drink of all classes. The poor drank it at all times, the more well to do drank it at breakfast and lunch but had wine with their evening meal. Several kinds of strengths were brewed and "prima", "secunda" and "tertia" were terms commonly applied to the different grades.

In the country beer was made on the estates as required, but in the towns the brewers were restrained for a time from making more than two kinds, "strong" and double", and the prices at which these could be sold were fixed by Law.

With the growth of the towns, the brewers became more important and their beer became an article to be taxed for revenue. At the beginning of the reign of King William the duty on strong beer was one shilling and threepence per barrel and the price charged by the brewers to their customers (who usually fetched it themselves from the brewery) was sixteen shillings per barrel. By 1694 the tax amounted to four shillings and ninepence per barrel on strong beer and one shilling and threepence on light beer.

Later there were taxes on malt and hops and the latter remained until 1862. In 1880 the system of taxation was changed again and remains substantially the same today. Tax is charged on the initial gravity of the wort before fermentation and is heaviest on the stronger beers. With the new system of taxation in England it became necessary to have a license to brew beer at home even for one's own consumption and this iniquitous inhibition of one's freedom even in the privacy of one's own home continued for more than 80 years. By the early 1960's many people were regularly or occasionally making small quantities of beer, but few could find an office able and willing to supply a license. The Customs and Excise Officers found it impracticable to enforce this law and, happily, in April, 1963, it was repealed. There is now no legal inhibition to the making of beer at home although, like wine and cider, it is of course illegal to offer it for sale, without possessing the necessary license.

Beer has been the subject of praise both of poets and authors of all generations from Chaucer through Shakespeare to Boswell and Burns and on to Belloc and Chesterton. It has also been the cause of great poverty and distress by those who have indulged to excess. As in all things the answer lies in moderation, especially in home-brewed beer which is so much stronger and headier.

Different barleys naturally produce different beers. The finest barleys are malted with special care and used exclusively for the strong light ales. These are always heavily hopped and fermented to dryness. They produce the bottled pale ales and draught beers. Other barleys are malted with subtle differences, dried at higher temperatures, sometimes roasted to near black and then, mixed in appropriate proportions, are made into bottled brown ale, draught mild, strong brown ale known as "old", and, of course, stout. In general the pale beers are stronger and drier, and the darker beers just a little less strong and slightly sweet to the discerning palate.

Barley is usually grown specially for the purpose, and in recent years much research has gone into developing new strains particularly suitable. A grain of barley is extremely hard and consists mostly of starch, packed in little granules by fibre walls. A grain of malter barley is soft and sweetish, so first the starch in the barley has to be converted into fermentable sugar by malting. This process appears to be extremely simple, but in fact is a highly skilled operation.

Within the grain of barley are two tiny enzymes known as cytase and diastase, and in the right amount of warmth and moisture the cytase dissolves the fibre (known as cellulose) protecting the barley granules and the diastase then converts the starch to fermentable sugar. The difficulty, of course, is determining the right amount of warmth and moisture and here the skill of the maltster is needed. His decision depends on the quality of the grain and the precise purpose for which it is to be used. Basically, the barley is soaked in water for 60–70 hrs. until sufficient moisture has been absorbed to start the grains growing. The grain absorbs water to 50% of its own weight.

It is then spread on floors to a depth of 1–3 ft. depending on the weather and its age in a temperature of 54° F. (12° C.) and the germination is allowed to continue until the shoot, or to be precise, the acrospire, has grown to about three-quarters of the length of the grain. By this time the cytase has softened the hard cellulose sufficiently to enable the diastase to convert the starch into sugar, but the young plant has not yet grown sufficiently to use up any of the starch itself.

At this stage the maltster stops further growth by allowing the temperature to rise to 70° F. (21° C.), thus drying off the grains before lightly cooking them in a kiln. As already stated, the finest barleys are reserved for the bitter and pale ales, and so the grains are only lightly kilned so that both the colour and the delicate flavour are retained. Most of the grains, however, are dried at a slightly higher temperature to give malts of a fuller flavour and deeper colour, and they are used for the popular mild ales and stouts. Other malts are specially treated to give even more flavour and colour.

Brown malts are kilned over a wood fire so that the smoke can play its part in the treatment. Crystal malts are cooked in a gas oven. Some grains are roasted almost black and a proportion of them are used in making stout.

Before the malt is used in the brewery, the grains, now called grist, are passed through steel rollers to crush them, hence the phrase "grist to the mill". They are then put into a mash tun —an enormous iron vessel with a slatted false bottom— and the water is run in at a temperature between 148° and 155° F. (64–68° C.) depending on the type of beer being brewed. This is the moment of "mashing".

Water, known in brewing circles as "liquor", is a most important ingredient in making beer. As has already been stated, breweries were originally built all over the country, but as time went on only those breweries survived which produced the best beers. It was noted that these breweries were collected in certain areas and it was realized that the water from the local wells was the cause of the high quality of the beer. The notable example was at Burton-on-Trent, which has been known as the Beer Town of England. The well water was analysed in 1879 and found to contain measurable quantities of seven different salts, ranging from common salt to gypsum.

Gypsum plays a very important part in the making of beer. During the boiling of the wort, it separates out certain classes of nitrogenous matter in the malt and these are easily filtered off with the spent hops, thus assisting in the clarification of the final beer. When the contents of the Burton water were known and the reasons for the high quality of the beer understood, brewers everywhere else were able to adjust their liquor accordingly. Nowadays, most brewers use ordinary tap water, which is of a high standard of purity, and appropriate additions are made as required; hardening for bitters and pale ales and softening for dark ales and stouts.

During mashing the starch is washed out of the malt and the diastase already mentioned continues its process of saccharification until the starch has been entirely converted into wort sugars, known as dextrin, malt dextrin and maltose. Another enzyme known as peptase is also present and renders certain proteins soluble and these provide nutrient for the yeast, assist in flavouring and so on. Mashing takes only a few minutes, but the temperature is maintained for 4 hours by "sparging" and this is the most important part of brewing. The temperature is absolutely vital since even a variation of 1 or 2 degrees can alter the character of the brew. The enzymes are affected by the slightest change of temperature and the highly skilled brewer varies the temperatures he uses to make specific characteristics in the beer he is producing. During "sparging" hot water is sprayed on top of the floating grains, while the wort is drawn off from beneath.

Since 1880 brewers have used a proportion of sugar to raise the specific gravity of their wort. Some still use cane sugar which, as we have seen, can be converted by an enzyme in yeast, known as invertase, into a fermentable form. But most brewers use invert sugar, which is derived from cane sugar and is all ready for fermentation in equal portions of dextrose and laevulose. The argument is that it saves the enzyme from too much work! The dextrose is fermented quickly into alcohol and carbon dioxide, the laevulose more slowly, and it is the product of this second fermentation which puts the sparkle in beer. Some beers are also coloured with caramel, which as everyone knows is simply "burnt" sugar.

The wort is now pumped into an enormous copper vessel, heated with steam pipes, and hops are added in the proportions of ¼ oz. per gallon to ½ oz. per gallon, according to the type of beer being made. Hops and wort are now boiled together for 2 hrs. and for five reasons:

1. To stabilize the wort as prepared in the mash tun; this is

achieved by killing the enzymes in the high temperature of boiling.

2. To sterilize the wort by killing any unwanted bacteria, wild yeasts and moulds which may have been in the malted barley.

3. To extract the flavouring and preservative portion from the hops. These are the essential oils and the bitter resins, both found in the sticky yellow powder known as "lupulin" in the ripe hop cone.

4. To concentrate the wort to the specific gravity required.

5. To coagulate the more complex protein substances so that they can be filtered out.

After boiling the hops are allowed to settle for up to ½ hr. and then the wort is drawn off through them, as through a filter bed. It is then quickly cooled in a heat exchanger to about 60° F. (16° C.), and the yeast is added in the proportion of ½ oz. per gallon. The yeast is obtained from previous fermentations and consists of several strains of the cultivated saccharomyces cerevisiae. Some of these strains are better for fermenting the sugar, a process known as attenuation, others ferment quickly or slowly depending on their strain. These yeasts also divide themselves into two classes known as "top" and "bottom" yeasts, depending upon whether they collect during fermentation at the top of the vat, like the kind mostly used in England, or at the bottom as mostly used on the Continent. The wort is fermented for three or four days, surplus yeast being skimmed off from time to time.

The beer is now racked into casks, and some more hops and sometimes some more laevulose are added. The dry hops give additional flavour to replace any lost during boiling, and the sugar provides for a further fermentation in the cask to impart that foaming head so much admired in a glass of beer. After 4 or 5 days in barrel some "finings" are stirred in to clarify the beer. It is then allowed to stand again for a day or so to settle before being drawn off.

While this account may appear to be very full, it is in fact extremely brief, and numerous important details have necessarily been omitted. Nevertheless, if the brewers' processes are understood in general terms, they can the more easily be applied in the home.

It must be appreciated, however, that while an extremely palatable and wholly satisfying beer can be brewed at home, it will not compare exactly with that produced in a brewery. The minute variations in water and temperature, the effect of quantity and so on will produce inevitable variations. This is not to say that the beer produced at home will be inferior in quality, but it will possess slightly different characteristics.

For those who wish to malt their own barley, it is suggested that they should consult one of the many books on the subject. It must be remembered that malting is a highly skilled task, needing great knowledge of the botany and chemistry of barley grains, especially when they are in the presence of moisture and warmth. Some people may know where they can buy barley already malted and ground, and it is of course quite easy to buy malt extract from any drugstore. Some druggists also sell hops, and they can also be obtained from wine and beer making stores. Sugar presents no difficulty and while "lager" culture yeasts are readily available, they are somewhat expensive, unless you propose to culture them on for regular use. The ordinary baker's yeast is perfectly suitable for the odd gallon or so. It is almost certain to consist mainly, and perhaps exclusively, of saccharomyces cerevisiae, which is undoubtedly best for beer. If the water in your neighbourhood is very soft you may add up to 70 grains (4½ grams) of gypsum, which the druggist will call calcium sulphate. But most wine and beer making suppliers offer for sale a packet of special salts for adding to beer liquor. It should be remembered that hard water is best for pale and bitter beers, and soft water for mild and brown ales and stout.

To brew a gallon of beer at home, you will require a large pot and a fermenting vessel, both a great deal larger than the quantity of beer being brewed. Into the boiler put 10 pts. of hot—but not boiling—water, adjusted if necessary, then add the contents of a 1 lb. jar of extract of malt, ½ lb. of cane sugar, 1 oz. of hops and a large teaspoonful of caramel. Bring to the boil and continue to boil vigorously for at least an hour. The vigorous boiling is necessary to extract all the goodness from the hops, and to prevent the hops from burning on the bottom of the pot. In due course, strain the liquor from the hops into the fermenting vessel, and if necessary, increase the quantity of wort to 1 gal., or alternatively when the liquor is cold— 60° F. (16° C.)—check the specific gravity. Aim at a reading of 1·045–1·055° F. and if the reading is above this then add sufficient cold boiled water to reduce the gravity as necessary.

1 lb. of malt and ½ lb. sugar in a gallon of water should give you a specific gravity reading around 1·048. With the wort at 60° F. add ½ oz. of yeast granules, preferably creamed to a liquid consistency and "started" with a little malt and tepid water. A cloth should be laid over the vessel to exclude dust. The fermentation should begin almost at once, and within a few hours the wort will be protected by a creamy head of froth. In a day or so this head may be 2 ins. deep and so a glazed crock or polyethylene pail capable of holding 1½ gallon is excellent for a 1-gallon brew.

Two days after adding the yeast, skim off to within ½ in. of the wort and stir thoroughly to admit additional air. After 5 days the first fermentation will be complete and the specific gravity reading will be about 1·005–1·008. This is because not all of the sugars, notably the dextrins and malt dextrins, are readily fermentable and remain to give body and flavour to the beer. Finings may be added at this stage and up to ½ oz. of hops, say 8 or 9 of the flowers. The dry hops will add essential oils which may have come off with the steam during boiling. Let the beer stand for 24 hrs., then rack into clean dry bottles and add a teaspoonful of sugar to each bottle. This should preferably be added in liquid form by dissolving 8 teaspoonfuls of sugar in a little of the beer, and then sharing this syrup among the various bottles you are using. These must be of a crown cap type to effect a perfect air seal. Ordinary corks are useless. The sugar will cause further fermentation and this will add the necessary sparkle and head to your beer when you come to pour it out. This should be done very carefully so as not to disturb the yeast sediment. Keep the beer in bottle for at least 1 week, and if possible for 3 weeks, then serve at about 60° F. This is a cross between a mild draught beer and a bottled brown ale.

A bitter beer is made similarly, but for 1 gal. use 1 lb. of sugar instead of ½ lb., 2 ozs. of hops and no caramel at all. Aim at a specific gravity of 1·055. After fermentation prime with additional sugar, bottle and store for at least 2 weeks before drinking and serve slightly colder—55°–60° F.

Stout is also made in the same way as other beers, but of course with soft water. Use 4 ozs. of roasted malt grains as well as the 1 lb. of extract of malt and ¾ lb. sugar with 1½ ozs. hops. Add double the quantity of sugar when bottling to give a really lively head and keep for 10 days or more.

"Milk" stout can no longer be bought under that name,

because the name implies the inclusion of milk in the beer, whereas there is only an addition of milk sugar known as lactose. This is not fermentable by any yeast and so remains as a sweetening. It can be bought from the drugstore and may be added to a stout beer to suit your taste when bottling, in addition to the cane sugar of course. It is suggested that 4 ozs. of lactose to the gallon might well be adequate for most palates.

Lager beer can also be brewed at home, but use only ½ oz. hops per gallon and no caramel. Ferment at a temperature of about 50° F. for 3 days and then reduce the temperature to 40° F. until fermentation ceases, which may be anything up to six months. You should, of course, use a lager yeast culture for this purpose. This yeast ferments from and settles on the bottom of the fermenting vessel. The beer will have light dry flavour and should be served at about 40° F.

Although it is not easy to come by, especially in small towns, some people may be able to obtain barley already malted. If it isn't ground then it must be rolled with a rolling pin to crack the grains. As has already been stated the temperature at which the malt is mashed plays a decisive part in determining the quality of the beer, and home brewers with access to malt grains may be wondering how they can overcome this problem. The solution is remarkably simple and effective.

Use a 2-gal. polythene pail with a lid, or a similar vessel. Heat 1¾ gals. of water to 150° F., pour it into the bucket and add 2 lbs. of crushed malt. Then insert a 50-watt glass immersion heater, put the lid on the bucket or vessel, cover with a blanket or the like to keep the heat in, switch on the electricity and leave for 6 hrs. With this quantity of malt and water the heater will give a fairly constant temperature of just below 150° F., and excellent extraction of malt will be obtained. This little heater is not at all expensive and will last for years if handled and stored with care. It can be used in conjunction with a thermostat, but used in the manner described the thermostat is quite unnecessary.

After the 6 hours' mashing, strain the liquid into a pot, add 3 ozs. hops and boil for one hour to extract the hop flavours. Strain into a fermentation vessel and add 2 lbs. of invert sugar, like the brewer, or 2 lbs. of cane sugar and a tablespoonful of caramel for darkening if required. Add sufficient cold water to bring the total quantity of wort up to 4 gals., cover with a thick cloth or polyethylene sheet and allow to cool. Cream 2 ozs. brewer's yeast or baker's yeast granules with half a pint of the wort, which has been cooled quickly by swirling in a jug, and allow this 2 hrs. to get started, before adding it to the bulk of the wort. Fermentation will be vigorous and much new yeast will be formed, most of which should be skimmed off on the second day.

Allow the fermentation to work out before bottling and prime each bottle with a little syrup as already indicated. Store for 1 week till the beer is clear, and serve cool but not cold.

Chapter 25

CIDER AND PERRY

THERE IS a long history of cider-making in England, although the early records are few. It seems clear that cider was made by the Ancient Britons during and possibly even before the Roman occupation, and there are reasons to believe that at the time of the Norman Conquest there was a long tradition of cider-making, especially by the Celts in the West of England. In 1205, during the reign of King John, we find the first written record, and the regular making of cider from specially planted trees continued and thrived during the next 450 years. By the middle of the seventeenth century there were many books and treatises on the subject—the classic work being written in 1656 by a Dr. Beale. At this time there were notable orchards in the counties of Hereford and Gloucester, a little further south in Devon and Somerset and over in the south-east in Kent, the traditional Garden of England.

Fifty years later, cider drinking began to decline as gin drinking increased and consequently cider-making was largely discontinued and the art was practically lost.

In 1890 some public-spirited gentlemen set about the restoration of cider-making. Old orchards were pruned and sometimes dug up and replanted. County Education Committees were later interested in developing this aspect of country life and subsequently the University of Bristol opened a research station at Long Ashton, where scientific study could be made to develop the most suitable apples and the best methods of cider manufacture.

Cider is the fermented juice of apples and theretically any apples may be used. In practice, however, experience teaches us that certain apples are most suitable than others and those which give the best results are in fact useless for eating either raw or cooked. These apples are of four main types although there are a number of varieties, with slightly different characteristics in each type.

The four types are: sweet, bitter sweet, bitter sharp and sharp. The best cider is made from a blend of the best quality apples in each type and develops an indescribable "vintage quality". From this lofty pinnacle there are many satisfying ciders slowly descending into "rough cider" which, though excellent in the field for a hot and thirsty palate under the noonday sun, lacks the finesse needed for the dining table or the lounge.

Almost three-quarters of an apple consists of juice which can be obtained first by crushing and then by pressing the pulp. It may be said at the outset that unless you have at least a *small* press, cider-making is an extremely laborious task. The crushing presents no serious problem since, after mellowing, the apples can be washed, cut up and put through the mincer, or simply washed and then mashed in a wooden tub or plastic bucket with a masher or balk of wood. Since the apples are usually wind-falls it is important to wash them thoroughly before crushing them. They can be mellowed by allowing them to stand a few days in a dry place until the skin can be dented when pressed with a fingernail.

The pulp is next placed in a cloth and pressed. With even a small press this task is not difficult, but without some mecha-nical aid, there is "no joy in the job". The best that can be suggested to you in these circumstances is to use a large poly-ethylene bag about 60 × 24 ins. Put your crushed pulp into a perfectly clean burlap sack or the like, and tie the neck securely. Place this in the plastic bag, lay a plank of wood on the two and, while holding up the mouth of the bag, stand on the wood and rock steadily to and fro. From time to time empty out the juice and keep on rocking until you are exhausted! The remains left in the sack may be used as compost in the garden and the juice can now be fermented in much the same way as wine. Depending on the success you have with pressing, 20 lbs. of apples will give you between a gallon and a gallon and a half of juice.

Of that 20 lbs. of cider apples it is suggested that a suitable blend will be obtained from 10 lbs. of medium sharp, 5 lbs. of sweet and 5 lbs. of bitter sweet. If you know where to get real cider apples you will be able to get local advice on the blending of the particular varieties available to you. If you have to use cooking and dessert apples, try 5 lbs. Bramley Seedlings (which are very sharp), 10 lbs. any dessert apple such as Blenheims, Orange Pippins or Worcester Pearmains, and 5 lbs. crab-apples. The latter can usually be obtained without much difficulty since many people grow the tree for its ornamental beauty rather than its fruit. Naturally this blend of cooking, dessert and crab-apples will not produce as good a cider as if you used proper cider apples, but it is well worth a try.

When all the juice has been extracted, strain it into a fermentation jar and measure the specific gravity by using your hydro-meter. If the reading is below 1·045 then enough sugar must be dissolved in some of the juice and added to the whole to bring the figure to at least 1·045, but not above 1·060. The addition of 2¾ ozs. of sugar per Imperial gallon will raise the gravity by 5 degrees. Next, test for acidity by tasting or as previously described. If it tastes very sharp, leave it alone. If it doesn't, then add one Campden tablet to the gallon. More precisely, aim at an acid content of 0·45%. If the figure is higher, the acid will take care of any bacteria that may be present and the malo-lactic fermentation will subsequently take care of the acid taste. If the figure is below 0·45% it will be necessary to add one Campden tablet to the gallon of juice to kill the stray bacteria certain to be present on the fruit. All this of course is very similar to winemaking. Apples usually possess enough natural yeast nutrients and plenty of tannin, the latter being especially abundant in the bitter varieties. Nevertheless it is a safeguard to add one nutrient tablet to the gallon of juice to ensure a good ferment.

Left alone, the juice will be fermented by the wild yeasts present on the fruit—saccharomyces apiculata. The ferment will be short and frothy and produce only 3% or 4% alcohol. It is better to use a normal pure yeast starter of a variety suitable for general wine purposes, or better still, a champagne yeast. Ferment the fruit fairly slowly by standing the jar (complete with fermentation lock, of course) in a cooler rather than a warmer place. A temperature of about 60° F. (16° C.) will be found most suitable. The ferment will not be violent and the flavour will be improved because volatile esters and flavourings will not be carried away. On the other hand if the ferment is too slow, other organisms will have the opportunity to grow and this must be avoided.

If you have not yet decided on the kind of cider you wish to make, you must do so now. A sweet cider must be racked when the specific gravity has been reduced to 1·025 and if necessary again at 1·020 and 1·015· Each racking removes a good deal of the yeast and unless the juice was especially strong in nutrients the chances are that you have achieved a naturally sweet cider that is stable enough for bottling· A useful test is to stand a well-corked bottle three-quarters full of cider in a warm place— about 75° F. (23° C.)—for about 2 weeks. Then examine the quantity of yeast deposit in the bottle and note whether there is a rush of gas when you remove the cork. If there is much yeast and gas the cider is still rich in nutrient and yeast cells will continue to grow and ferment the sugar to alcohol and carbon dioxide after bottling. You can add two Campden tablets to the gallon to kill the yeast or you can ferment "on", making a stronger but less sweet cider. If there was little yeast deposit in the bottle and only a sparkle in the cider when you withdrew the cork, then you may rightly assume that all will be well when you bottle the bulk of your produce.

Crown cap bottles are best for bottling cider, for they make a sound air-tight seal which will enable sufficient pressure of carbon dioxide to built up for the cider to be lively and sparkling when served. Fill the bottles slowly and quietly, which means preventing the cider from splashing into the bottles. This retains the gas. For the same reason, store in a cool place and serve cool.

Not being high in alcohol content, ciders will not keep for very long without spoilage. Nevertheless, they should be matured for from 4 to 6 months. After 1 year they usually begin to deteriorate.

Dry cider is fermented for as long as necessary to use up nearly all the sugar. It is important that it should be racked when the specific gravity has been reduced to 1·010 to get rid of the dead yeast and other unwanted impurities. The cider will finish fermenting in bottle, thus producing a dry but sparkling drink.

To sum up then, mellow, wash, crush and press the apples already blended for sweetness, bitterness and sharpness. Add one Campden tablet per gallon if necessary. Ferment with a champagne or an all-purpose wine yeast. Rack both during and after fermentation. Bottle in crown cap bottles, mature, but drink within the year.

PERRY

Just as there are special apples used in cider-making, so there are special pears for making perry. They are grown mainly in the south-west Midlands in England, especially in Worcestershire, and the different varieties have a mixture of idiosyncrasies which make perry a difficult beverage for the amateur to make. Dessert or cooking pears are generally inadequate for perry production, even on a small scale, and if you can only obtain a supply of these you are advised to add sufficient sugar to increase the specific gravity to 1·100 and make a pear wine, using a champagne yeast and two teaspoonfuls or two tablets of yeast nutrient per gallon.

If you are sufficiently fortunate to be able to obtain some perry pears, then the farmer will no doubt be able to give you some advice regarding the varieties he has sold to you. Some varieties have to be crushed and pressed as soon as they fall from the tree, some require a period to mature before using. They must be perfectly sound when crushed, for any rottenness is noticeable in the finished perry. Other varieties are very high in tannin content, and the crushed pears have to be allowed to stand for several hours before pressing so that some of the excess tannin may precipitate. When the juice is pressed add two Campden tablets per gallon, check the specific gravity and adjust it if necessary between 1·045 as the minimum and 1·070 as the maximum. Check the acidity and add the juice of a large lemon if necessary. Add nutrient and yeast and ferment till the specific gravity has fallen to 1·025, which is about as low as it is desirable to go. The flavour of perry is very delicate at the best of times and is lost without a background of sweetness. Sometimes perry is slow to clear and it is often necessary either to add a fining or to filter through asbestos pulp.

Chapter 26

GINGER BEER, ETC.

MANY PARENTS allow their children one small glass of wine occasionally, and experience shows that the children rapidly become discriminating, declining wines they do not like while their parents accept all that is offered to them! Certain drinks are, however, firm favourites with children—notably, of course, ginger beer—and we feel that this book would not be complete without some information and recipes on this subject.

For the past few summers, the ginger beer plant craze has swept the country. Once started one must go on producing ginger beer every week or until one finds the courage to say "no more".

The ginger beer plant occurs in various forms in different generations. Older folk will remember "Bee Wine" which in some places was known as "Beasty Wine" (perhaps they dropped the "l"!) or Californian Bee Wine.

Basically a ginger beer plant looks like a brown sludge in the bottom of a jam jar, half filled with water and loosely covered. The accompanying instructions provide for the daily addition of 1 tablespoonful of sugar and 1 of ginger, stirred in till the sugar is dissolved. After 7 days the juice of 2 large lemons must be added and stirred in. The liquid is then strained into a large vessel; 8 pts. of water, ½ lb. of sugar and the thinly peeled rinds of the lemons are added, stirred in and the vessel covered. After 2 days the liquid must be bottled, corked and the corks tied well down, and left for not more than 2 weeks. The brew is delicious to some and disliked by others. It should be served cold on a hot day, if it is to give of its best. There is some, but not much, alcohol present and a good deal of carbon dioxide to make the drink fizz when it is poured out.

The brown sludge has to be divided after the straining. One half can be used to start the next brew, the other half can be given to someone else or thrown away. To start the brew again you add ¾ pt. of cold boiled water, 1 tablespoonful of sugar and 1 of ground ginger, stir thoroughly, cover and leave in a warm place.

Upon examination of the sludge, biologists found that the ferment was caused by a complex combination of a yeast known as saccharomyces pyriformis together with harmless bacteria.

154

The yeast is, of course, in a sense a plant and the ground ginger added daily for flavouring provides the popular name "ginger beer plant".

Inquiries among your friends will no doubt provide you with a plant for nothing, but a culture with full instructions can be bought from winemaking supply houses.

A more orthodox recipe for a well-flavoured ginger beer is as follows:

GINGER BEER

	Imperial	U.S.	Metric
Well-bruised ginger	1½ oz.	1¼ oz.	45 grams
Cream of tartar	½ oz.	½ oz.	15 grams
White sugar	1 lb.	14 oz.	½ kilo.
Water	1 gallon	1 gallon	5 litres

Thinly pared rind and juice of 2 lemons.
Packet of granulated bakers' yeast.

Put the ginger, cream of tartar, sugar and lemon rinds in a vessel and pour on 1 gal. of boiling water. Stir thoroughly to dissolve the sugar, cover and leave the brew to cool. Then add the lemon juice and sprinkle on the yeast granules. Closely cover again and leave in a warm place for 24 hrs. Remove any scum, siphon into bottles (avoiding screw stoppers) and mature for 3 days. Serve cold and beware of the fizz. We would emphasize that it is HIGHLY dangerous to use screw stoppers, this ginger beer being so gassy. One or two people have had nasty accidents with burst bottles, but this can be avoided by using corks, which will either "blow" or can be seen straining at their ties.

ORANGE SQUASH

Another simply made drink for children is as follows:

	Imperial	U.S.	Metric
Sugar	2 lb.	1¾ lb.	1 kilo.
Citric acid	¾ oz.	¾ oz.	20 grams
Magnesium sulphate	½ oz.	½ oz.	15 grams
Tartaric acid	1 oz.	1 oz.	30 grams
Boiling water	1½ pints	1½ pints	1 litre

Juice and thinly pared rind of 4 large oranges.
Colouring.

Mix all the ingredients together in a vessel, cover and leave overnight; bottle and use diluted to taste. This is an extremely good orange squash costing no more than half the shop price.

Parents with young children often find that a bottle of fresh fruit cordial is a wonderful tonic in winter when appetites tend to wane. All the soft fruits and the stone fruits too are excellent for this purpose. First the juice has to be extracted and this is most effectively achieved by heating gently; then the juice is sweetened and bottled and the bottles must be sterilized and sealed.

To extract the juice the fruit can be placed in an enamelled or aluminum saucepan with just enough water to prevent the fruit sticking to the bottom. Put the pan over a gentle heat and slowly bring to the boil. Meanwhile the fruit should be stirred frequently and broken up with a wooden spoon. Once boiling-point has been reached the pan should be removed from the heat and the liquid strained from the pulp.

A somewhat safer method is to use a double saucepan with plenty of water in the bottom pan, or an ordinary china basin in any sort of pan containing water. The basin should be raised from the bottom of the pan by sticks of wood or the like. A tablespoonful of water should be added to the fruit, which should be mashed with a wooden spoon and heated long enough to extract all the juice.

A jelly bag, nylon sieve, or linen cloth should be used for straining, and the pulp should be squeezed until it is as dry as can be obtained. ¾ lb. of sugar should now be added to each pint of fruit juice, but if the juice is especially sharp, up to 1 lb. of sugar per pint may be used. Stir the juice thoroughly until the sugar is completely dissolved, and it is a good idea to check this by straining once again.

The syrup should now be bottled for sterilizing. This kills all yeasts and bacteria and ensures that the syrup will keep pure and wholesome till it is required. Coloured, screw-stoppered bottles are best for a perfect seal and to preserve the colour of the syrup. Place the filled bottles in a saucepan or fish kettle, protecting the bottles from the direct heat on the bottom of the pan. Put the stoppers in the bottles but leave them loose so that steam and air can escape during the period of heating. Fill the pan to the necks of the bottles. Bring the water to boiling point, then simmer for 20 mins. Remove the bottles and stand them on a piece of wood, hold each one in a thick cloth and screw the stopper down as tightly as possible.

When the bottles are cool, tighten the stoppers again, label and set aside for the winter. There is no point in retaining them after the fresh fruits become available again. Some fine pulp which passed through the straining cloth may settle on the bottom of the bottle, but the bottle should not be opened until the contents are required. The sediment has no effect either way. The syrup can be poured carefully off the lees or shaken up, just as you wish.

The juice can be diluted with water, either hot or iced, or with soda water. Milk can also be used as long as it is chilled first and stirred briskly while the syrup is added slowly. This prevents curdling. The syrup should be diluted 5 or 6 times for drinks, but may be used neat in jellies, ice creams and suitable puddings.

VINEGARS

No careful winemaker should make vinegar accidentally, but it is obviously simple to make deliberately. In small quantities fruit vinegars can be a very useful ingredient to have in the kitchen. The must should have a specific gravity of about 1·050; some malt vinegar should be added in the proportion of 5 parts fruit must to 1 part vinegar.

Half fill a glass jar and plug the neck with cotton wool. Stand the jar in a very warm place, about 90° F., and leave for 6–8 weeks. At a lower temperature up to twice this time may be needed. When the liquid has acquired a full vinegar flavour and has an acetic acid content of 4% or more, bottle the vinegar, cork and seal securely. Store till the vinegar is clear, although this may take 8 or 9 months. Siphon into clean bottles and add a solution of Campden tablets in the proportion of two tablets to 1 gal. of vinegar. This keeps the vinegar free from infection while in use.

Raspberries, blackcurrants and blackberries make excellent vinegars. Use 3 lbs. of fruit, 1 lb. of sugar, 100 oz. water and 20 oz. of vinegar.

Chapter 27

ASSOCIATIONS OF WINEMAKERS

ALTHOUGH WINEMAKING is such an ancient art, the formation of clubs to study it, and its subsequent growth as an "organized" hobby, is quite recent—since 1953, in fact.

In England that year, sugar came "off the ration"—how long ago it all seems now!—and many people found themselves able to resume their winemaking, or to venture upon it for the first time. Consequently in many areas winemaking started again, "old hands" at the craft found themselves pressed to reveal their recipes and "know-how", and there was a demand for information on the subject.

The first Winemakers' Circle in England was formed at Andover, in Hampshire, in January 1954, as the result of some recipes for home-brewed beer which had been published in the local newspaper's Christmas Supplement. The three founders had had a friendly meeting as a result of this and, quite by chance, came round to wondering whether anyone else would be sufficiently interested, as they were, to pursue their studies further. They thought it would be worth finding out, so they published in the paper an invitation to anyone interested to meet at a certain restaurant at a given time and place. Little did they know that they were setting a pattern for a movement which was to sweep the country.

There was an excellent response and in January 1954 the Andover Amateur Winemakers' Circle was formed. Quite independently, and without any knowledge of this, winemakers in other parts of the country were doing the same, and within a matter of months a Winemakers' Guild was formed at Welwyn Garden City and an Amateur Winemakers' Association was formed at Cheltenham. At Andover the name "Circle" was chosen, typifying the friendliness and compactness it was hoped to foster; elsewhere the title "Guild" was preferred, as being particularly applicable to a skilled craft.

Fundamentally the Circles are certainly similar to the ancient English Guilds in that they include those whose knowledge and experience would rate them the rank of a master winemaker. There are many with sufficient experience to rate them journeymen and there are many coming forward as apprentices. Furthermore, as of old the purposes of the Guilds are to keep alive this country's tradition of winemaking, to assist their members to improve the standard of their craft and to help beginners.

The clubs spread quite slowly at first, but the early ones did some proselytizing and sponsored others in nearby towns and then, in December 1957, the first issue of *The Amateur Wine-maker,* a magazine devoted exclusively to the hobby, appeared, and there was an immediate upsurge of interest. Circles could see what their companions elsewhere were doing, and many winemakers hitherto working in isolation were inspired to form their own groups, so that by the end of 1964 over 200 were in existence and the idea had spread throughout England, into Scotland and Wales and even overseas.

Most guilds meet once each month at an agreed time, date and place. A small entrance fee is charged and an annual sub-scription. Speakers are invited to address the members on subjects to do with the making of wine, mead, cider and ales or to give practical demonstrations. Time is allowed for the ex-change of ideas by discussion and for tasting each other's wines.

Members are taught the principles of appreciation and jud-ging from time to time special assessment forms are issued and members taste half a dozen wines and try to assess their qualities and defects.

An economic aspect is that facilities can be provided for the ready purchase by members, often at a reduced rate, of the necessary equipment, jars, labels, corks, capsules, yeasts, etc., etc.

In addition to the activities mentioned, Circles sometimes ar-range outings to places of interest to winemakers, and organize a Christmas party so that the members can relax from learning and simply enjoy their wines.

The more experienced winemakers find that they are some-times called upon to talk at Women's Institutes, Townswomen's Guilds and similar societies. Their services are also claimed as judges by Horticultural or Floral Societies, who include classes for wines ar meads made at home in their programme. This work is undertaken with joy because it often brings new mem-bers to the craft of winemaking, as well as to the winemakers' societies.

These include among their members men and women from the professions, administrative and clerical posts, business men and women and tradesmen, as well as those whose work has no high-sounding title, such as the housewife interested in every aspect of homecraft. Irrespective of social position, members meet on a common ground with a common interest, and new rich friendships are quickly formed; a glass of wine is a great "leveller"! Everyone has something to learn and everyone has something to give.

The most common entrance fee appears to be half a crown with an annual subscription of 10s. for one person or 15s. for husband and wife. Perhaps because making wine in the home is such an ancient tradition, the majority of members are husbands and wives, and share the activity and pleasure together. All winemakers are strongly recommended to seek out and to join their local Guild. If there is as yet none in your neighbourhood, you might well consider forming one. It is amazingly simple to form a Circle and anyone doing so will find great satisfaction in his or her endeavour.

First have a word with your local newspaper editor and arrange for him to include a paragraph about the venture in his gossip column. You will find him most friendly and co-operative. Alternatively, you can write a letter to the Editor, briefly explaining your proposal and asking anyone interested to write to you. You can expect up to two dozen or more replies. Or you can insert an advertisement in the paper giving the time, date and place of a meeting to which all are invited and wait for them to turn up.

When booking a room for the evening, have consideration for those who may have to come some little distance and make your rendezvous as central as you can. Avoid school premises and large halls if possible, because their atmosphere just isn't conducive to a friendly discussion about wine. It is a great help if you can find a comfortable, well warmed and pleasingly decorated room capable of holding some 50 or 60 people.

At the first meeting perhaps 20 or 30 will be present and you can outline the purposes for forming a Guild or Circle that we have already given, and after a little discussion, decide to form one and determine your meeting place and time. The amount of the admission fee can be fixed and the annual subscription discussed. This figure should be kept as low as possible, but nevertheless should be sufficient to cover the cost of hiring the room each month, to allow something for postage and stationery and enough to make a small offering to your Speakers.

Try to organize your next meeting before you disperse. Many

of those present are likely to be very inexperienced and might appreciate most a general talk on how to make a particular wine appropriate to the time of the year. You can perhaps undertake this yourself or persuade one of the more experienced members to do so.

At the next meeting, after you have got to know each other a little better, you will need to elect a Chairman, Secretary and Treasurer for the first year. The Secretary will form a register of names and addresses and the Treasurer can begin to collect the fees. After the talk the Chairman should allow opportunity for discussion and ideas for future meetings should be elicited. Perhaps two or three members could join the officers to form a working committee. As you progress you will find many little plans to be made and it is better for these to be arranged by a small committee than to occupy the time of the general meeting, when members will not wish to be bothered with administrative details. They want to get on with the task of tasting and talking about ine. You might also find it an advantage to elect a President to represent you on certain occasions and to be the continuing figurehead at times of elections. He or she should be someone of personality, with gifts of leadership and diplomatic authority in time of crisis. The honour should not be lightly bestowed and the privilege should be treated with great respect by the person elected.

As soon as possible a programme should be planned and published for the coming twelve months and adhered to as far as possible; the Secretary writing to invite speakers and the Treasurer providing facilities for the purchase of equipment by the members.

There seems little point in keeping formal minutes at the general meetings, though it is useful to keep them of the committee meetings.

The Secretary should circulate a leaflet—it can be stencilled rather than printed—setting out the objects of the Guild, the meeting place, date and time, the fees and subscriptions and the programme for the year. This will be found very useful to give to enquirers and new members.

Keep the meetings as simple as possible, allow plenty of time for questions and be very kind to any member asking for an opinion on their first wine. Perhaps your first attempts weren't quite so good either!

There is much to be said for the small Circle or Guild, where everyone knows everyone else. Once the membership gets much beyond 70 or 80 it is difficult to keep the meeting informal and friendly. If there are so many potential members, then form another group. And don't put out too much paper. If a circular is sent out each month giving news and recipes there is a likelihood that the attendance will drop even if the membership increases. Much of the success so far has been due to the wonderful, friendly atmosphere created by the members actually present. Try to keep it that way.

Chapter 28

EXHIBITIONS, COMPETITIONS
AND JUDGING

Throughout the country there are annual fairs, floral and horticultural shows at which it is becoming increasingly popular to stage exhibitions of wines made by members of a Guild, and sometimes when facilities for judging can be provided there are competitions as well. These activities are of great benefit, setting a steadily improving standard, and they greatly increase interest in our craft. The range of varieties and colour shows up well in an exhibit of modern country wines. Invariably the wine stand is one of the most popular in the show, and draws envious glances from other exhibitors!

Let us suppose that your Circle has been invited to have a display stand at the local autumn fair (it always happens, sooner or later!). Usually the job of actually arranging the stand will be given to one or two of the most artistically inclined members, but all members will have some contribution they can make, apart from wine—sign-writing, card lettering, equipment, wine novelties, special lighting, flowers, greenery, and so on. Incidentally, it is well worth while, if you have some "handymen" amongst your number, to design a semi-permanent stand which can be easily assembled and dismantled, and which will allow a maximum of effective display; it is best made so that it can be adapted to one, two or three of the normal 6-ft. folding tables commonly encountered. This does save an enormous amount of work at future shows.

All members, of course, will contribute wines for display, and care must be taken to obtain a good range of wine of all possible colours. Deep reds (in clear bottles for once) look most attractive, and concealed lighting behind the bottles enhances their appearance greatly. The bottles will be delivered to a central collecting point the day before the show, or to the show itself very early on the day, and the "window-dresser" *must* be allowed ample time, far more than would be thought necessary. It is best to have one reliable and artistic person in sole charge whose word on arrangement is law; with two or three people all trying to put their own ideas into practice, chaos (and arguments!) soon develop.

Before submitting a wine for an exhibition make sure that it is freshly racked and absolutely brilliant, with no trace of haze in the wine and no deposit in the punt. Use proper wine bottles principally for exhibiting your wine, clear for white and brown or green for red. A few fancy bottles and novelties are welcomed by the "window-dresser" but should be used sparingly. At all costs avoid fruit juice bottles, sauce bottles and the like. It is obvious to everyone what they are and that they are being used as a makeshift because you haven't obtained proper bottles, and they do let our craft down badly in the eyes of the knowledgeable. Most hotel keepers are glad to get rid of their empty wine bottles, so that there is no difficulty about the supply. Make sure that the bottle is absolutely clean inside and out and under the punt as well. See the chapter on Hygiene if you need to refresh your memory on how to do this. Drain and shake the bottle till it is dry, then fill the bottle to within 1½ ins. of the top of the neck. Cork tightly and finish with a flush top either by using a cork stopper or cutting off any protrusion of a cylindrical cork. Next fit a capsule, either of tinfoil or plastic, and make sure that its colour is in harmony with the colour of the wine and the label. Prepare a label, either produced by your own club or bought commercially, to indicate the type of wine, and the date it was made, e.g.

PARSNIP WINE
February
1964

Print this as boldly and clearly as you can in Roman or Gothic script, using a strong black ink. The label should be stuck on the front of the bottle, i.e. equidistant from the two seams half-way up the bottle or just a little higher. Finally, give the bottle a polish with a clean cloth to remove any fingerprints, and wrap in tissue paper for delivery to the exhibition stand.

If you are the "window-dresser", concerned with setting out the stand, first see that you have a "backdrop" as well as a table. Obviously this will depend on the local circumstances, but a useful idea is to have a trellis made up with a "backcloth" of crepe paper or material. Black is always effective for this and burgundy and gold are worth considering. The trellis can be painted white. Somewhere the name of the Guild should be prominently displayed and this could be at the top of the trellis. Hung on the woodwork could be fruits, flowers, leaves, root vegetables and the like. Some publications should be displayed and from the artistic point of view it is best to choose books and journals with bright or bold jackets or covers.

Try to construct the stand around a theme, and devise one or two arresting features for it. You can show a wine in all its stages or concentrate on wines suitable for the occasion, e.g. at the flower show, exhibiting a collection of flower wines as the centre-piece with perhaps some blooms in vases among the bottles. At a horticultural show a range of vegetable or fruit wines could be raised up and singled out, with the fruits and roots shown too. Beer can be shown fermenting, and the vinegar fly and apparatus will make other items too. These are no more than suggestions upon which you can readily improvise and improve. It is always helpful if you can have something to give away, a leaflet about your Guild, or simply a recipe "written up" and duplicated. It is very worth while to have someone always in attendance to answer questions and to keep an eye on things; depend upon it, there will be no lack of questions, the attendants will be kept hard at it.

COMPETING

Preparing wine for a competition is slightly different. First and foremost you must comply strictly with the rules governing the competition as regards types of bottle, filling, labelling, etc. Make sure that you enter in the right classes, being careful not to put a sweet wine, even accidentally, in a dry wine class, or vice versa. Don't be afraid to put several entries in the same class, if the rules allow, rather than to pick the one that you think is best. The judge is only human and has likes and dislikes different from yours. The wine that you reject as being not quite your best according to your taste, may be the very one the judge concerned thinks the best of the show. These considerations apart, prepare your bottle only a day or two before the entry on the lines already discussed for exhibiting wine.

ORGANIZING

If you are invited to act as a judge you have a very responsible task and should take it very seriously. It is so easy to offend people unintentionally through carelessness or lack of consideration.

A competition of any sort must obviously be governed by rules which will ensure that all entrants have an equal chance, and if you are one of the organizers you may find yourself with the task of drawing them up. Wine Circles, too, often receive requests for advice on wine classes from horticultural shows. You may also find yourself invited to judge, in which case it is always as well to be able to give advice as to how the competition should be organized and what rules are necessary. It makes your job much easier on the day!

Remember, however, that it is quite impossible for any judge to cope with a large class of mixed sweet and dry wines: once he has tasted a really sweet wine his palate is destroyed for a dry one; any dry wines which he tastes afterward will seem over-astringent or even acid, though they may be excellent wines and far better than the over-sweet one. Remember also that a judge should not be asked to appraise more than 40 or 50 bottles of wine at any one time, and that to do this adequately will take two to three hours of concentrated attention.

In planning your programme then, try to estimate how many bottles of wine may be expected and make sure that you allow sufficient judges and sufficient time in which to judge the wines.

To sum up: bear in mind the remarks just made, draw up in tabular form the schedules and rules of your show, and circulate them well in advance of the chosen date. Word them in a clear direct style quite free from ambiguity. Include the names of the judges so that exhibitors will know that their wine is going to be properly appraised. Set as high a standard as you think it possible to achieve. Provide suitable labels, so that all bottles can look the same and so sensure that there is no possibility of the judges being able to recognize an exhibit from the label on the bottle.

You should specify where the labels are to be stuck on the bottles, and it is useful to have two labels, one stating the number of the class and the number of the entry and the second label the name and year of the wine; no other information whatsoever should be permitted.

For competitions, organizers might like to consider the following rules as a working basis, to be added to at will:

1. The schedule of classes shall be as follows:
   (You should now set out the classes you have decided to include.)

2. 26-oz. colourless wine bottles only may be used.

3. Cork stoppers must be used.

4. Only the labels provided may be used. The class and entry label shall be attached ½ in. from the bottom and the name and year of the wine 1 in. from the shoulder. No other mark or printing must appear on either bottle or label.

5. All bottles will be opened and sampled.

6. Entries to be received by such and such a time. Bottles to be delivered by (such a time) to (such and such a place).

7. An entry fee of (so much) a bottle shall be paid prior to submission to cover the cost of organization.

8. No judge may enter the competition.

9. The competition organizers will be the sole arbiters of any question involving the interpretation of these rules.

10. No competitor will be allowed in the judging room while judging is in progress.

11. The judge's decision shall be final.

12. Certificates of merit will be awarded for the first, second and third best wines submitted in each class.

13. The results shall be made known at (such a time).

14. No bottle may be collected by an exhibitor before (such a time).

15. The fact of entry in this competition implies acceptance of these rules.

At the actual show you should provide adequate tables upon which the bottles of wine are to be displayed. The tables look best when covered with white paper or plastic and if there are enough entries each class should have a separate table. The class title should be boldly displayed on each table together with an injunction not to touch the exhibits. Bottles can so easily be knocked over and broken.

If possible a small separate table should be temporarily provided at which the judge and the steward can work. Water and a vessel should be available for rinsing the glasses and another vessel for use as a spittoon.

While the actual judging is in progress no exhibitor should be allowed in the room. This cannot be over-emphasized. It secures the essential atmosphere of integrity and earns the respect of all those concerned.

When the awards have been made by the judges, all the bottles should be labelled with details of the winemaker and, where relevant, the nature of the award. The labels should be prepared beforehands and either stuck on to the bottles or, if on thin card, propped against the appropriate bottle.

It is a good idea to have the judges available for a while after the show is open to answer the questions of exhibitors. Stewards should be provided to ensure the care and safety of the bottles, since some exhibitors show the same bottle of wine in several different competitions. They would naturally be terribly upset if any calamity befell a prize-winning bottle of wine.

JUDGING

Having organized the competition side of the business, you must now consider the judges. In the first place no judge should be asked to consider more than four dozen bottles. In a big competition this would mean at least one judge for each class. In a small show perhaps the one judge could consider the dry wines and another the sweet, but we repeat, *no one person should be asked or expected to judge both dry and sweet wines on the same day.* If it is possible, also have assistant judges to enable the judge to compare opinions on a wine. This has the advantage, too, of giving training and experience to those just beginning the art of judging, for it must be realized that this is an art and that it is difficult to give paper guidance.

On page 171 we set out a model wine judging sheet which can be used.

As will be seen from a study of this judging sheet, a good wine must have a pleasant and enjoyable bouquet and aroma and an invigorating and delightful taste in the mouth. There can be a remembrance of the source of origin in the taste, but in fine wines this is sometimes extremely difficult to trace. Naturally it should have an alcohol content appropriate to its type and be sweet or dry according to its class. It should possess "body", which can perhaps be defined as texture, or substance. The wine should also possess sufficient astringency or "bite" and sufficient, but not too much, acid. All must be in balance.

Ability to classify these characteristics in a wine is the first step towards judgment; the ability to compare degree of characteristics is the art which separates a good judge from a poor one.

Other factors, apart from the wine itself, are of course also considered by the judge; the appearance of the bottle, label and cork, the clarity and brilliance of the wine, must all be given some reward. The judge will hold the bottle to the light to study the colour of the wine and will need to examine the wine in a glass. He will swirl the contents to bring out the bouquet and note the glycerine adhering to the side. He will sniff it both gently and vigorously and then take a good mouthful to chew around in his mouth while he considers his comments.

Obviously then at a show each judge will need two or three glasses, a bowl of warm water for washing them and some tea towels for drying them. He will need a corkscrew to remove corks and a penknife or pliers to remove capsules or cut the wire of corks that have been tied down on sparkling wines. He will need mark sheets and a pencil or two. To do these menial but necessary tasks someone should be found to help him.

Most of all, however, and this is a MUST, he should have provided for him some little cubes of cheese or dry bread or plain biscuits to cleanse his palate after tasting each wine. If this were not provided the poor judge would find that, after tasting only three or four wines, his palate had completely gone and all wines would taste the same.

There is diverse opinion as to whether prizes should take the form of money or goods or just certificates. We feel that there is much to be said for the honour of winning to be expressed in the form of a certificate, for it is the knowledge that he or she has won or been awarded a place that is the real prize. If it is felt that something more tangible should be given, then this could perhaps take the form of one or more wineglasses, of which one can never have enough.

After the competition a spokesman for the judges could well make a general statement about the entries, with perhaps individual comment about the winning wines. He would be unwise to go further and his decision must clearly be final and admit of no discussion.

So much for actual competitions. But wine Guilds can have much fun and teach their members something of the art of judging in a similar way. From four to six bottles of wine (preferably on one evening dry wines and on another sweet wines) are prepared for judging, the plate of biscuits and cheese not being forgotten. Each member present is then given a mark chart and tries his hand at judging the wine. It is astounding how similar will be the verdicts. If an experienced member can then give a commentary—so much the better.

A simple chart for this purpose is as follows:

Marks

Appearance of bottle, label and cork (Presentation)	4
Clarity and colour	8
Bouquet	8
Taste and texture	40
Total	60

The following chart will be found to be very helpful in learning the business of judging. Although it is in great detail, for more so than would be used in actual competition, it is most useful in teaching what to look for and how to be systematic in judging. The point breakdown can be adjusted to ones preference.

WINE JUDGING SHEET

CLASS .... JUDGE ....

DISQUALIFY: (*a*) Exhibits in Wrong Class
(*b*) Exhibits Not According to Schedule
(i.e. in wrong type bottles or wrongly labelled)

	Points	Possible Points	Exhibitor's Entry No.								
1. PRESENTATION											
Cork: clean and of good quality (1)											
Bottle: clean and sound (1)											
Airspace: Should not exceed ¾" (1)											
Label: Legible (1)											
Affixed squarely midway between seams of bottle, at correct height		4									
2. CLARITY, COLOUR											
(*a*) Hazy, wine, or											
Wine with FLOATERS or esasily disturbed sediment	0										
(A firm sediment that does not lift on pouring is allowable, particularly in a red wine)											
(*b*) Clear wine	2										
(*c*) Bright wine	4										
(*d*) Starbright wine	6										
Good colour, add	2	8									
3. BOUQUET											
Attractiveness	3										
Vinosity	2										
Degree of development	2										
Suitable for purpose of wine	1										
Off odours? (deduct marks)		8									
4. TASTE & TEXTURE											
(Flavour, quality and general impression)											
General flavour	10										
Balance	10										
(sweetness, acidity, astringency, bitterness)											
Vinosity	10										
General impression including:											
Apparent alcohol content (whether suitable for wine's purpose) and/or Suitability for purpose (in "wines by use" class)	10										
Deduct marks for:											
Acetification											
Off flavour (from whatever cause)											
Bacterial infections											
Oxidation (except in oxidised wine classes)											
Instability (in still wine classes)		40									
		60									

These marks are in exactly the same proportions as those recommended by the National Guild of Judges but are doubled to allow of an easier split-down of Section 1. They will therefore give similar results.

Chapter 29

EXTRAS FOR THE HANDYMAN

A GREAT DEAL of pleasure can be obtained by making and using equipment that is a real help, but the cost of which, if bought commercially, would be prohibitive for most of us. The following suggestions are offered, not so much to be slavishly copied, but rather as ideas to be adapted and developed according to your abilities and resources.

FERMENTATION FACILITIES

It is not always easy to find a suitable place in a small house where fermentation jars can be left for months at a time, and sometimes garages, sheds or greenhouses are pressed into service. Unfortunately the temperature in such places is not always conducive to fermentation, especially during the winter months. For the odd jar or so, especially if it is a largish one of 4 gals. or even more, it is possible to use an immersion heater and thermostat. The heater and thermostat are of the sort used in aquariums. The jar should be well wrapped to avoid heat loss, and by this method fermentation can be continued in a shed even during frost or snow. This is particularly important with mead, which ferments slowly for a very long period, often all through the winter.

Another useful idea is a fermentation cupboard and this has the obvious advantage that several jars can be fermenting at the same time. The cupboard may be built to your own specification in the space available, or an existing cupboard can be adapted for the purpose. The shelves need to be far enough apart to hold at least a gallon-sized jar, complete with fermentation lock. It is important too that the shelves be slatted, or that a number of holes be drilled in them for warm air to circulate. The heat can be provided from an infra-red tube about 2 ft. long and 2 ins. in diameter. The tube should be fitted on the floor of the cupboard beneath the first shelf, while the thermostat, which you can set to control the heat as desired, should be fitted centrally. The door should be well fitting, or the heat will escape.

A tea chest can also be used. Two wood strips 2 × 1 × 18 ins. are screwed to sides opposite each other and about 8 ins. up from the bottom of the box so that they form a ledge on which a slatted shelf can be fitted. A square of peg-board, to which have been screwed two or three wood strips 2 × ½ in. and long enough to rest on the ledges, will do nicely. Four 1-gal. jars will just fit in the box, which should be supplied with a well-fitting lid complete with handle.

Beneath the shelf an infra-red tube can be screwed to the floor of the box and a small hole should be drilled to enable the cord to pass through. This is a perfectly safe set-up, but if you wish, a thermostat set at 68° F. (20° C.) may be set in a corner of the upper chamber. (See Fig. 14, p. 92).

An item of equipment which every winemaker would like to possess is a wine press; unhappily, at $60 or so, it is far too expensive for many people to buy. If you can afford one it is well worth having, for it takes a lot of the hard work out of extracting the juice from fruit. It is also far better than simply squeezing a cloth by hand, no matter how strong your hands. Page 92 shows two commercial presses, well made, simple to use and throughly recommended. For those winemakers who would rather make their own press for a few dollars and several hours' carpentry, we offer the following two suggestions. The wood can probably be obtained as ends at any lumber yard and a car jack can usually be used for the screw.

1. Basically this press consists of a tray to which a box is fitted. A screw provides pressure on a block which fits inside the top of the box. The size of the box can be anything from 6 ins. cube upwards to about 10 ins. The tray should be a couple of inches larger all round. Adjust your size according to the materials you can obtain. There is no need to copy these arbitrary measurements.

The tray is 12 ins. square with a surrounding ridge 2 in. high. An opening is cut to let out the juice into a vessel to be placed beneath. For material you can use: hardwood, Formica, or softwood, provided this is lined with an adhesive plastic covering. Make sure the coverage is adequate and sound in the joints and also around the opening. A shallow wedge on the bottom of the tray, opposite the outlet, will provide a gravity flow for the wine in the direction required.

The box is designed cube-shaped instead of cylindrical for simplicity in manufacture. Four pieces of hardwood, such as oak or ash, are needed. Two pieces are cut wider than the other two so that a simple butt halved joint can be used. The carpenter/winemaker will no doubt use the superior dovetail joints, which, if well made, will need neither glue, screws nor dowels to hold them firm. For the rest of us a high degree of efficiency can be obtained from the simple joint already mentioned. Before jointing them drill a number of holes in the lower half of each side, through which the juices can flow, as with a colander. If you can, drill at an angle so that the juice flows down to the tray. As many holes as you like can be bored so long as the wood is not weakened. The sides should be at least ¾ in. thick. They can be joined with ½-in. dowels about 1½ ins. long driven tight into drilled holes. Three will be needed for each corner. Additionally L-shaped angle irons must be put around the corners to hold them firm against the pressure. But paint the metal with two coats of enamel paint before use and use chromium-plated screws. Along the top of opposite sides of the box attach, with long stout screws, two brackets shaped like suitcase handles, but much smaller.

The only part of this, or any other press, which might be difficult to obtain is the threaded rod and nut. A hardware or garage owner will usually be found helpful—if you tell him what you are doing. All that is wanted is a metal bar about 10 ins. long, 1½ ins. wide and ¼ in. thick. In the centre a drill a suitable hole, then braze a nut over this. The threaded rod passes through the nut. A cross bar can be welded at the top end of the rod.

Finally, make a substantial block to fit inside the box as closely as possible. It needs to be at least 1 in. thick and may be covered all over with a sheet of adhesive plastic. On the top, fix in the centre a metal plate, if possible with an open cup fitting, to take the lower end of the screw.

When this is done attach the box to the tray by wooden dowels, three to each side. Make a good tight fit and knock them in firm and flush.

When you are ready to use the press, put the fruit or pulp into a linen cloth, place it into the box, lay the block on top of the cloth, insert one end of the metal bar into one of the brackets screwed to the edge of the box, and slide the other end of the bar into the other bracket. Now screw steadily and slowly. Wait till the juice stops flowing before increasing the pressure and continue until the pulp is dry and no more juice can be extracted. *It is a mistake to apply too much pressure too quickly.*

Before using, wipe over all the surfaces likely to come into contact with the wine with a cloth dipped in a solution of potassium metabisulphite. After using the press, wipe it thoroughly clean as before using, and finally, dry off with a clean cloth.

2. Rather less elegant, but tremendously strong, is a press designed rather like a picture frame. Four stout pieces of wood 2 × 2 ins. are joined in the form of a square and strengthened at the corners with angle iron bolted onto the frame. In the centre of one side a hole is drilled and a metal nut is inserted and this side is regarded as the top. The opposite side is the bottom and to this is screwed a stout tray of 1-in. thick wood with 2-in. sides and blocks at each end to maintain the balance. A box and lid as described in model 1 rests in the centre of the tray, for the strain is taken by the frame. An outlet for the juice is made at one end of the tray and the block beneath the outlet may be ½ in. less thick to ensure a flow.

Chapter 30

CHOOSING THE MOST SUITABLE YEAST

MOST WINEMAKERS start off by using granulated baker's yeast and there is no doubt that this is cheap, easy to obtain and easy to use. After some experience, however, most people graduate to sedimentary wine yeasts in culture, liquid or tablet form.

It cannot be emphasized too much that the choice of yeast is dictated not so much by the principal ingredient from which the wine is being made as by the type of wine which it is desired to produce. One might make several brews from the same batch of fruit, and, by varying the sugar content and using a different yeast in each, produce several widely differing wines.

But the ingredients used do have some bearing on the choice of yeast, in that certain fruits lend themselves to the making of one sort of wine rather than another.

For first attempts the beginner would be well advised to play for safety, and use a "general purpose" wine yeast (indicated in the table as "G.P.") for all wines, thus becoming accustomed to the use of cultures and starter bottles, and to the flavours of popular ingredients.

With more experience you may wish to experiment further, and inevitably thoughts will turn to the production of sherry, port, Sauterne, and champagne type wines. It is then that you will need to employ quality yeasts.

It is important, first of all, to consider whether the wine is to be sweet or dry, and whether it is to be still or sparkling, for this will govern not only the choice of yeast but also the amount of sugar which is to be included.

In making your choice you will find it helpful to bear these basic facts in mind:

For dry red wines, a Pommard yeast is excellent, but we suspect that they are more to the popular taste if made slightly sweet with a port or burgundy yeast. If you intend to fortify a wine and to have it sweet, try a port, Malaga or Madeira yeast.

For sweet dessert wines choose a Sauterne or Tokay yeast, and for all your table wines (whether white or red) you can use a general-purpose wine yeast. This will also make a satisfactory mead, although some advocate the use of Maury yeast.

176

For sherry type wines, whether sweet or dry, use a sherry yeast, of course, which is also good with several of the root wines.

Flower wines generally have a delicate flavour and aroma, and most experts prefer to retain these undiminished by using a general-purpose yeast.

For sparkling drinks (champagne-type wines, cider, perry, elder-flower, champagne, etc.) choose a champagne yeast, or a Herrliberg.

Beers and ales are best made with brewer's yeast or with granulated baker's yeast or Carlsberg Lager culture.

Grapes, of course, will make any type of wine. Richly coloured red fruits like elderberries, blackberries and damsons lend themselves to the making of port types, or burgundies, strong-flavoured fruits like raspberries are best used for sweet wines, bilberries and sloes are good for dry red wines, rhubarb and gooseberries for sherries and sparkling wines, and apples and parsnips for sherry-type wines, both sweet and dry. Pears will make an excellent Sauterne-type wine, and plums are best used for the production of sweet wines. Of the flower wines the queen is elderflower, either still or sparkling, with may blossom a good second, hile dandelion will make an excellent sweet wine.

Where several yeasts are listed, they are given in order of preference, but that is not to say that your preference will be the same. There's only one way to find out—try them when opportunity arises!

AGRIMONY—G.P.
APPLE—G.P., Sherry, Champagne
APRICOT—Sherry, G.P.
BALM—G.P.
BARLEY—Sherry, G.P.
BEER—Brewer's, Lager (or Carlsberg), G.P.
BEETROOT—G.P.
BILBERRY—Bordeaux, Burgundy Port, G.P.
BIRCH SAP—G.P., Champagne
BLACKBERRY—Port, Burgundy, G.P., Sherry
BLACKCURRANT—Burgundy, Sherry, G.P.
BRAMBLE TIP—G.P.
BROOM—G.P., Sherry
BULLACE—G.P.

BURNET—G.P.
CARROT—Sherry, G.P.
CELERY—G.P.
CHAMPAGNE (ELDERFLOWER) —Champagne, Herrliberg.
CHERRY: Black—Bordeaux, G.P.
Red—Bordeaux, G.P.
Morello—Bordeaux, G.P.
CIDER—Champagne, Herrliberg, G.P.
CLOVER—G.P.
COLTSFOOT—G.P.
CORN—Sauterne, Madeira, G.P.
COWSLIP—G.P.
CRAB-APPLE—G.P.
CRANBERRY—Burgundy, G.P.
CURRANT—Sauterne
DAMSON—Port, Malaga, Madeira (Sweet), Pommard (dry)

DANDELION—G.P., Sauterne (sweet), Burgundy
DATE—Sherry
ELDERBERRY—Port, Burgundy, G.P., Malaga
ELDERFLOWER—G.P., Sautrne, Tokay
ELDERFLOWER CHAMPAGNE—Champagne, Herrliberg
FIG—Sherry
GINGER BEER—G.P.
GINGER WINE—G.P.
GOLDEN ROD—G.P., Sherry
GOOSEBERRY—Champagne, Tokay, Sauterne (sweet), Sherry
GRAPE—Any wine yeast according to desired result
GRAPE SYRUP—Any wine yeast according tao desired result
GRAPEFRUIT—G.P.
GREENGAGE—G.P.
HAWTHORN BERRY—G.P.
HAWTHORN FLOWER—Sauterne, G.P., Tokay
HOP BEERS—Brewer's, Lager (Carlsberg), G.P.
HOREHOUND BEERS—G.P.
LEMON—G.P., Sherry
LETTUCE—G.P.
LIME BLOSSOM—Sauterne, Tokay, G.P.
LOGANBERRY PORT—Burgundy (dry), Sauterne (sweet),G.P.
MAIZE—Sauterne, Madeira, G.P.
MALT—Brewer's, G.P.
MANGOLD—G.P., Sherry
MARIGOLD—G.P., Sauterne
MARROW—G.P., Sherry
MAYBLOSSOM—G.P., Sauterne

MEAD—G.P., Maury
MULBERRY—Port, G.P.
OAK LEAF—G.P.
ORANGE—G.P., Sherry
PANSY—G.P.
PARSLEY—G.P., Sherry
PARNIP—Sherry, G.P.
PEAPOD—G.P.
PEAR—G.P., Sherry, Port
PLUM—Bordeaux (dry), Sauterne, Tokay (sweet), Sherry (sweet), Pommard
PLUM (DRIED)—Malaga, Madeira
POTATO—G.P.
PRIMROSE—G.P.
QUINCE—G.P.
RAISIN—Tokay, G.P.
RASPBERRY—Burgundy, Port, Sauterne, G.P.
REDCURRANT—Burgundy, G.P.
RHUBARB—Sherry, Sauterne, Champagne
RICE—Sherry, G.P.
ROSE-HIP—Sherry, G.P.
ROSE-PETAL—G.P.
ROWANBERRY—Sherry, G.P.
SLOE—G.P., Burgundy
SPINACH—G.P.
STRAWERRY—Sherry
SUGAR BEET—G.P., Sherry
TEA—G.P., Sherry
VANILLA—G.P.
VINE PRUNINGS— Any wine yeast
WALNUT LEAF—Sherry
WHEAT—G.P., Sherry
WHITE CURRANT—Tokay, Haut Sauterne, G.P.
WHORTLEBERRY—G.P.

Chapter 31

RECIPES

T HE RECIPES which follow are not meant to be more than
basic examples, which you can vary to suit your fancy. The
information given in the preceding chapters will enable you to
alter these basic recipes in accordance with the ingredients you
have available at the time.

A number of recipes are given for dried fruits, dried flowers,
grain and concentrated grape juice. The great advantage with
these ingredients is that the wine can be made at any time during
the year to suit you convenience. Consequently they can sometimes receive more care in the making than certain fresh fruits
which demand urgent attention at specific times. In the past
these wines have received very little attention from winemakers,
who have tended to regard the summer season as their busy
period. With the knowledge now available different wines can
be made all the year round and this is a very real advantage to
the winemaker who likes to play tennis on summer evenings.

In the reference to sugar, quantities are given for cane or
beet sugar. If invert sugar is used, one-fifth more must be used,
as invert sugar contains 20% water. Therefore, instead of 2½
lbs. of cane sugar you should use 3 lbs. of invert sugar. Furthermore it should be remembered that 1 lb. (½ kilo.) of sugar takes
up the space occupied by 10 fl. oz. (300 ml.) of water. As all
the recipes require 1 gal. or 5 litres of water it will be obvious
that the total quantity of must produced will be more than sufficient for this size jar. The excess should be fermented in a
bottle beside the jar, and used for topping up, during fermentation if necessary but more particularly after racking, when a
small amount of wine is inevitably lost with the lees.

FLOWER WINES

Every experienced winemaker will agree that flowers give a
wine exquisite bouquet and flavour. Many would agree that elderflowers make the queen of wines, while the names cowslip, coltsfoot and dandelion wines justifiably enjoy a superb reputation.
Unfortunately very few city dwellers are ever able to gather
these country flowers fresh from the fields, and as a result these
wines are not made nearly as frequently as others less attractive.

Experiment has shown that dried flowers make excellent substitutes. Accordingly, wherever possible, dried flowers are offered as an alternative to fresh, and with this information those unable to gather fresh flowers may well be able to make and enjoy these lovely wines.

Remember that flowers have little to offer a wine apart from bouquet and flavour. Therefore acid and tannin should be added to the must, and of course sufficient nutrient salts for the yeast. If you wish to make a dessert wine from flowers you should add ½ lb. (250 g.) of coarse chopped raisins to the fermenting must in addition to the sugar.

The method is similar for all flower wines. To save repetition the details will be given in tabulated form below, and only the quantities and any special note will be given under the names of the flowers.

Method

1. Fresh flowers should be gathered on a dry sunny day when the petals are fully open.

2. The tiny florets and larger petals should usually be picked from the calices so that no green parts are included in the must. The green imparts an unpleasant bitterness to the wine and is best omitted.

3. Place the flowers in a mashing vessel together with the thinly pared rinds of 2 oranges and 2 lemons.

4. Pour on 1 gal. or 5 litres of boiling water, or bring the flowers and cold water to the boil, as may be necessary.

5. Cover the vessel and leave for 3 or 4 days while the essences are extracted.

6. As the flowers will float on the surface of the water, they should be pushed down twice daily with a wooden spoon and stirred about.

7. Strain off the liquor and press the pulp until it is dry.

8. Add 3 lbs. (1½ kilo.) of sugar, raisins if required and the juice of the oranges and lemons, a teaspoonful or 1 crushed tablet of nutrient salts and the yeast starter.

9. Stir gently but thoroughly till the sugar is completely dissolved and then pour the must into a fermentation jar.

10. Fit an air-lock and ferment in a warm room.

11. When fermentation is finished, rack into a storage jar and add 1 dessertspoonful of cold strong tea or ¼ teaspoonful of grape tannin.

12. Rack again in 3 months and for the third time 3 months later still.

AGRIMONY

1 fair-sized bunch of fresh agrimony, or 1 packet of dried agrimony. 2 ozs. (60 g.) of bruised root ginger may be added after fermentation if you like your wines slightly "hot". Gently boil the agrimony and rinds for 20 mins., strain onto the other ingredients but do not add the yeast till the must is cool.

BROOM

1 gal. of broom flowers, or 1 packet of dried broom. Gently boil the broom and rinds for 20 mins., strain onto the other ingredients but do not add the yeast till the must is cool.

CLOVER

1 gal. of purple clover blossoms, or 1 packet of dried clover flowers. Pour the boiling water over the flowers and steep as recommended, strain, add other ingredients and ferment.

COLTSFOOT

1 gal. of coltsfoot flowers, or 1 packet of dried flowers. Pour the boiling water onto the flowers and steep as recommended. Strain, add other ingredients and ferment.

COWSLIP

1 gal. of cowslip flowers, or 1 packet of dried flowers. Use only the yellow petals and pour the boiling water over them and steep as recommended. Strain, add other ingredients and ferment.

DANDELION

2 qts. (2½ l.) of dandelion heads, or 1 packet of dried flowers. Pour the boiling water on the flowers and steep as recommended. Strain, add other ingredients and ferment.

ELDERFLOWER

1 pt. (¾ l.) of well-pressed-down fresh florets, or 1 packet of dried flowers. Pour the boiling water onto the flowers and steep as recommended. Strain, add other ingredients and ferment.

GOLDEN ROD

2 handfuls of blossoms, or 1 packet of dried flowers. Pour the boiling water onto the flowers and steep as recommended. Strain, add other ingredients and ferment.

HAWTHORN OR MAY BLOSSOM

2 qts. (2½ l.) of fresh hawthorn flowers, pink or white. Pour the boiling water onto the flowers and steep as recommended. Strain, add other ingredients and ferment.

MARIGOLD

1 gal. (5 l.) of fresh marigold heads, or 1 packet of dried flowers. Pour the boiling water onto the flowers and steep as recommended. Strain, add the other ingredients and ferment.

PRIMROSE

1 gal. (5 l.) of fresh primroses. Pour the boiling water onto the yellow petals and steep as recommended. Strain, add other ingredients and ferment.

OAK LEAF

1 gal. (5 l.) of oak leaves picked as soon as fully grown but while still young, i.e. in late June. Rinse in cold water to

remove dust and then drain. Pour on boiling water, steep as recommended, add other ingredients and ferment. The tannin should be omitted after racking as the leaves contain sufficient. These leaves may also be added to other wines as flavouring.

ROSE PETAL

2 qts. (2½ l.) strongly scented dark red rose petals, pressed well down. Pour boiling water onto the petals and steep as recommended. Strain, add other ingredients and ferment.

VINE PRUNINGS

5 lbs. (2½ kilo) of vine leaves and young tendrils, provided they have *not* been sprayed with a copper preparation, such as Bordeaux mixture. Pour on the boiling water and steep as recommended. Strain, add the other ingredients and ferment.

WALNUT LEAF

1 large handful of walnut leaves picked, rinsed and drained as for oak leaves. Pour on the boiling water and steep as recommended. Strain and add other ingredients, but using demerara sugar or some honey or raisins to give added body. Ferment.

FRUIT WINES

Fruit juice is contained in minute cells by pectin and this has to be broken down before the juice can be extracted (p. 79).

After crushing the fruit, the pulp needs to be soaked for 2 or 3 days so that pectinase can destroy the pectin.

Alternatively, the fruit pulp may be slowly heated to about 160° F. (71° C.) for a short time and then pressed, or Pectozyme may be added as indicated earlier to do the work of the pectinase.

The first method is the one most strongly recommended.

Although the fruit may have some wild yeast on its skin, we recommend without reservation the use of a good wine yeast, properly prepared as previously indicated. The addition of a yeast nutrient is equally necessary for the best results.

APPLE WINE

	Imperial	U.S.	Metric
Apples (mixed varieties)	12 lb.	10 lb.	6 kilo.
Crabapples (optional)	1 lb.	1 lb.	½ kilo.
Campden tablet	1	1	1
Sugar	2½ lb.	2 lb.	1¼ kilo.
Water	1 gallon	1 gallon	5 litres

Yeast and nutrient.

Method:

Wash the apples, removing any parts that are rotten, and cut up small. Dissolve the Campden tablet in the boiling water and pour over the apples. Stir twice each day for 10 days, but keep the tub closely covered meanwhile. Strain off the liquor and press the pulp in a cloth to extract the remaining juice. Stir in the sugar, nutrient and yeast, and ferment.

APRICOT WINE

	Imperial	U.S.	Metric
Fresh apricots	6 lb.	5 lb.	3 kilos.
Water	1 gallon	1 gallon	5 litres
Sugar	3 lb.	2½ lb.	1½ kilo.

Yeast and nutrient.

Method:

Stone the apricots and cut up the fruit. 3 or 4 stones may be broken and the kernels added to impart the suggestion of an almond flavouring. Pour the boiling water over the fruit and steep for 2 days, strain, add the sugar, nutrient and yeast, and ferment.

APRICOT WINE (DRIED)

	Imperial	U.S.	Metric
Dried Apricots	12 oz.	10 oz.	400 grams
Water	1 gallon	1 gallon	5 litres
Sugar	3 lb.	2½ lb.	1½ kilo.

Yeast, nutrient and two lemons.

Method:

Cut up the apricots and soak them overnight in cold water. Next day strain and boil the pieces for 15 mins. Strain onto the sugar, stir well, cover and when cool add the lemon juice, nutrient and yeast, and ferment.

BANANA WINE

	Imperial	U.S.	Metric
Peeled bananas	4 lb.	3½ lb.	2 kilo.
Banana skins	½ lb.	½ lb.	250 g.
Raisins	¼ lb.	¼ lb.	125 g.
Sugar	3 lb.	2½ lb.	1½ kilo.
Water	1 gallon	1 gallon	5 litres

Yeast, nutrient, 1 lemon, 1 orange.

Method:

Very ripe, spotted or black bananas are quite suitable. Put the bananas and skin into a linen bag, place the bag into a saucepan of water and bring to the boil. Gently simmer for 30 mins., then strain onto the sugar and stir well. When cool, add the orange and lemon juice, and squeeze the bag to extract as much liquid as possible. Finally add the nutrient and yeast, and ferment.

BLACKBERRY WINE

	Imperial	U.S.	Metric
Blackberries	8 lb.	6¾ lb.	4 kilo
Sugar	2½ lb.	2 lb.	1¼ kilo.
Water	6 pints	6 pints	3¾ litres
Campden tablet	1	1	1

Yeast and nutrient.

Method:

Crush the blackberries and Campden tablet and steep in the water for 2 days, stirring twice daily. Strain and press, add sugar, nutrient and yeast, and ferment.

BLACKCURRANT WINE

	Imperial	U.S.	Metric
Blackcurrants	3 lb.	2½ lb.	1½ kilo.
Sugar	3½ lb.	3 lb.	1¾ kilo.
Water	1 gallon	1 gallon	5 litres
Yeast and nutrient.			

Method:

Strip the fruit and rinse under the tap to remove odd bits of stalk, etc.; place them in a vessel, mash them with a wooden spoon and pour the boiling water onto them. Steep for 2 days, strain and press, add the sugar, nutrient and yeast, and ferment.

BULLACE WINE

	Imperial	U.S.	Metric
Bullaces	4 lb.	3½ lb.	2 kilo.
Sugar	3 lb.	2½ lb.	1½ kilo.
Water	1 gallon	1 gallon	5 litres
Raisins	8 oz.	7 oz.	¼ kilo.
Campden tablet	1	1	1
Yeast and nutrient.			

Method:

Pour boiling water onto the bullaces. Leave for 24 hrs; break them up with your hands, add Campden tablet and leave for 4 days, stirring twice daily. Strain the fruit and press, add the sugar, nutrient and yeast, and ferment.

CHERRY WINE

	Imperial	U.S.	Metric
Cherries (white, black, or best of all, mixed)	6 lb.	5 lb.	3 kilo
Include sour cherries, or juice or 1 large lemon.	1 lb.	1 lb·	½ kilo.
Sugar	2½ lb.	2 lb.	1¼ kilo.
Water	1 gallon	1 gallon	5 litres
Yeast and nutrient.			

Method:

Stalk and wash the cherries, removing bad ones. Pour on the boiling water and cover. When cool crush the fruit, re-cover and leave for 2 days. Strain onto the sugar, stir well until dissolved, then add nutrient and yeast, and ferment.

MORELLO CHERRY ALE

	Imperial	U.S.	Metric
Morello cherries	2 lb.	1¾ lb.	1 kilo.
Sugar	1 lb.	14 oz.	½ kilo.
Old ale, stout or home-brewed beer	3 pints	3 pints	2 litres
Yeast.			

Method:

Remove the stalks, wash the fruit and prick well with a needle. Dissolve the sugar in the beer and pour on the fruit, add the yeast and cover. After fermentation, strain well but do not crush the fruit, which can be used in tarts, trifles, etc.

DAMSON WINE

	Imperial	U.S.	Metric
Ripe sound Damsons	4 lb.	3½ lb.	2 kilo.
Sugar	3 lb.	2½ lb.	1½ kilo.
Water	1 gallon	1 gallon	5 litres
Yeast and nutrient.			

Method:

Stalk and wash the fruit, then pour on the boiling water and cover. When cool, crush the fruit with your hands and re-cover. Stir twice daily for 4 days. Strain and press the fruit and pour the liquid onto the sugar, add nutrient and yeast, and ferment.

DATE WINE

	Imperial	U.S.	Metric
Dried dates	4 lb.	3½ lb.	2 kilo.
Sugar	2 lb.	1¾ lb.	1 kilo.
Water	1 gallon	1 gallon	5 litres
4 lemons, yeast and nutrient.			

Method:

Chop the dates and boil gently for half an hour with the thinly pared lemon rinds. If possible include a dozen or so stones to increase the tannin content of the liquid. Strain onto the sugar, stir well and cover. When cool, add the lemon juice, nutrient and yeast, and ferment.

ELDERBERRY WINE

Elderberries, stripped and washed	4 lb.	3½ lb.	2 kilo.
Sugar	3 lb.	2½ lb.	1½ kilo.
Water	1 gallon	1 gallon	5 litres

Juice of 1 large lemon, yeast and nutrient.

Method:

Pour boiling water over the fruit, stir well, cover and leave for 4 days, stirring twice daily. Strain and press the juice onto the liquid onto the sugar, add nutrient and yeast, and ferment.

FIG WINE

	Imperial	*U.S.*	*Metric*
Dried figs	3 lb.	1¾ lb.	1 kilo.
Sugar	2 lb.	2½ lb.	1½ kilo.
Water	1 gallon	1 gallon	5 litres

2 lemons, yeast and nutrient.

Method:

Break up the figs with your fingers. Add the sugar and lemon peelings and pour on the boiling water. Stir well, cover, and when cool add the lemon juice, nutrient and yeast. Ferment on the pulp, stirring twice daily for 10 days; then strain and continue the ferment.

GOOSEBERRY WINE

	Imperial	*U.S.*	*Metric*
Gooseberries	6 lb.	5 lb.	3 kilo.
Water	1 gallon	1 gallon	5 litres
Campden tablet	1	1	1
Sugar	2½-3 lb.	2-2½ lb.	1¼-1½ kilo.
Grape tannin	½ tsp.	½ tsp.	½ tsp.
Yeast nutrient	1 stp.	1 stp.	1 stp.
Yeast.			

Method:

See Chapter 15, page 91.

GRAPEFRUIT WINE

	Imperial	U.S.	Metric
Grapefruit	8	7	8
Sugar	2½ lb.	2¼ lb.	1¼ kilo
Water	7 pints	7 pints	4½ litres
Yeast and nutrient.			

Method:

Peel the grapefruit thinly or grate the yellow rinds into a bowl. Cut the fruit in half and squeeze out the juice onto the rinds. Add the sugar and cold water and stir thoroughly. Add the nutrient and yeast. After 4 days, strain off the skins and continue the fermentation.

HAWTHORNBERRY WINE

	Imperial	U.S.	Metric
Hawthornberries	1 gallon	1 gallon	5 litres
Water	1 gallon	1 gallon	5 litres
Sugar	3 lb.	2½ lb.	1½ kilo.
Juice of 2 lemons, yeast and nutrient.			

Method:

Pour the boiling water over the berries, cover, and when cool crush, re-cover and leave for 4 days, stirring twice daily. Strain onto the sugar and stir till this has dissolved. Add the lemon juice, nutrient and yeast, and ferment.

LEMON WINE

	Imperial	U.S.	Metric
Small lemons	10	8	10
Sugar	3 lb.	2½ lb.	1½ kilo.
Water	1 gallon	1 gallon	5 litres
Yeast and nutrient.			

Method:

Thinly peel the rind from only half the lemons and add to the sugar. Pour on the boiling water, and when cool, add the strained juice from the lemons, the nutrient and yeast, and ferment.

LOGANBERRY WINE

	Imperial	U.S.	Metric
Loganberries	4 lb.	3½ lb.	2 kilo.
Sugar	3 lb.	2½ lb.	1½ kilo.
Water	1 gallon	1 gallon	5 litres
Yeast and nutrient.			

Method:

Pick over the berries to remove stalks. Pour on the boiling water, cover and when cool mash the fruit, cover and leave 2 days, stirring twice daily. Strain and press the juice onto nutrient and yeast, and ferment.

MIXED FRUIT WINE

	Imperial	U.S.	Metric
Mixed fruit: black or white or red currants, raspberries, cherries, gooseberries, etc. whatever is available	6 lb.	5 lb.	3 kilo.
Sugar	3½ lb.	3 lb.	1¾ kilo.
Water	1 gallon	1 gallon	5 litres
Yeast and nutrient.			

Method:

Clean the fruit, pour on the boiling water, cover and when cool mash the mixture. Re-cover and leave for 3 days, stirring twice daily. Strain and press the juice onto the sugar. Add the nutrient and yeast, and ferment.

MIXED DRIED FRUIT WINE

	Imperial	U.S.	Metric
Mixed dried fruits, sultanas, currants, raisins, etc.	2½ lb.	1¾ lb.	1 kilo.
Wheat	1 lb.	1 lb.	½ kilo.
Sugar	3 lb.	2½ lb.	1½ kilo.
Water	1 gallon	1 gallon	5 litres
2 oranges, 2 lemons, yeast and nutrient.			

Method:

Soak the wheat in cold water overnight, drain and crush, then mix with the dried fruit and sugar. Pour on the boiling water, stir well and cover. When cool, add the fruit juice, nutrient and yeast. Ferment on the pulp, stirring twice daily for 10 days, keeping the crock closely covered. Strain and press and continue the fermentation.

MULBERRY WINE

	Imperial	U.S.	Metric
Mulberries	8 lb.	6¾ lb.	4 kilo.
Sugar	3 lb.	2½ lb.	1½ kilo.
Water	4 pints	4 pints	2½ litres

Juice of 1 large lemon, yeast and nutrient.

Method:

Clean and rinse the fruit, drain, crush, add the lemon juice, sugar, nutrient, yeast and cold water. Cover, but stir twice daily for 4 days. Strain and press and continue the fermentation.

ORANGE WINE

	Imperial	U.S.	Metric
Seville oranges	5 lb.	4 lb.	2½ kilo.
Sweet oranges	5 lb.	4 lb.	2½ kilo.
Sugar	3 lb.	2½ lb.	1½ kilo.
Water	1 gallon	1 gallon	5 litres

Yeast and nutrient.

Method:

Thinly peel 2 of the Seville and 3 of the sweet oranges and add to the sugar. Pour on the boiling water and, when cool, add the juice from the oranges, the nutrient and the yeast. After 3 days, strain and continue the fermentation.

PEAR WINE

	Imperial	U.S.	Metric
Pears	6 lb.	5 lb.	3 kilo.
Sugar	3 lb.	2½ lb.	1½ kilo.
Water	1 gallon	1 gallon	5 litres

Juice of 2 lemons, yeast and nutrient.

Method:

Cut each pear into eight or more pieces and drop into boiling water. Cover and leave for 3 days, stirring twice daily. Strain and press onto the sugar. Stir well and add the lemon juice, nutrient and yeast.

PINEAPPLE WINE

	Imperial	U.S.	Metric
Four pineapples	4	4	4
Sugar	3 lb.	2½ lb.	1½ kilo.
Water	1 gallon	1 gallon	5 litres

2 lemons, yeast and nutrient.

Method:

Top and tail 4 fair-sized pineapples, slice them into a large saucepan or fish kettle, cover them with water, bring to the boil and simmer for ¼ hr. Strain onto the sugar, add the remaining water and stir well. Cover and allow to cool; then add lemon juice, nutrient and yeast, and ferment.

PLUM WINE

	Imperial	U.S.	Metric
Plums	6 lb.	5 lb.	3 kilo.
Sugar	3½ lb.	3 lb.	1¾ kilo.
Water	1 gallon	1 gallon	5 litres

Yeast and nutrient.

Method:

Cut up the fruit, pour on the boiling water, cover and leave 2 days. Strain and press the juice onto sugar, stir till dissolved, add the nutrient and yeast, and ferment.

PRUNE WINE

	Imperial	U.S.	Metric
Prunes	2. lb.	1¾ lb.	1 kilo.
Raisins	8 oz.	7 oz.	¼ kilo.
Sugar	3 lb.	2½ lb.	1½ kilo.
Water	1 gallon	1 gallon	5 litres

Yeast and nutrient.

Method:

Break up the prunes and raisins with your fingers, add the sugar and nutrient and pour on the boiling water. Stir well and cover. When cool, add the yeast and ferment on the pulp, stirring twice daily and keeping the crock well covered. Strain and press and continue to ferment.

QUINCE WINE

	Imperial	U.S.	Metric
Quinces	20	17	20
Sugar	3 lb.	2½ lb.	1½ kilo.
Water	1 gallon	1 gallon	5 litres

2 lemons, yeast and nutrient.

Method:

Wash the fruit and grate coarsely, but discard the cores. Bring fruit and water to the boil and simmer for 15 mins. Strain onto the sugar and add the rinds and juice of the 2 lemons. Stir well and cover. When cool, add the nutrient and yeast.

RAISIN WINE

	Imperial	U.S.	Metric
Raisins	4 lb.	3½ lb.	2 kilo.
Sugar	1 lb.	14 oz.	½ kilo.
Water	1 gallon	1 gallon	5 litres

Yeast.

Method:

Chop the raisins, add the sugar, pour on boiling water, cover, and when cool add the yeast. After a week, strain and press the raisins and continue the fermentation.

N.B. Raisins are best used with other ingredients. Alternatively add flavouring, such as a handful of elderflowers, before the water is added.

RASPBERRY WINE

	Imperial	U.S.	Metric
Fresh raspberries (no mouldy ones)	2½ lb.	2 lb.	1¼ kilo.
Sultanas	8 oz.	7 oz.	¼ kilo.
Sugar	3½ lb.	3 lb.	1¾ kilo.
Water	1 gallon	1 gallon	5 litres

Yeast and nutrient.

Method:

Pour boiling water onto the fruit and sugar, mash and cover. When cool, add the yeast and ferment on the pulp for 3 days, pressing down the cap twice daily. Keep carefully covered. Strain and press and continue fermentation as long as possible but finish with a sweet wine. The wine is not pleasant dry.

REDCURRANT WINE

	Imperial	*U.S.*	*Metric*
Redcurrants	4 lb.	3½ lb.	2 kilo.
Sugar	3½ lb.	3 lb.	1¾ kilo.
Water	1 gallon	1 gallon	5 litres

Yeast and nutrient.

Method:

Strip the currants and rinse in a colander. Pour on boiling water, mash with a wooden spoon, then cover and steep for 2 days. Strain and press, add the sugar, nutrient and yeast. Ferment as usual.

RHUBARB WINE

	Imperial	*U.S.*	*Metric*
Rhubarb	6 lb.	5 lb.	3 kilo.
Sugar	3 lb.	2½ lb.	1½ kilo.
Campden tablet	1	1	1
Water	1 gallon	1 gallon	5 litres

2 large lemons, yeast and nutrient.

Method:

Use garden rhubarb at the end of May. Remove leaf and trim the end. Wipe clean, chop or mince, add cold water and Campden tablet. Leave for 3 days, stirring twice daily. Strain and press the fruit dry. Add 1 oz. (30 grams) of precipitated chalk; when the fizzing subsides, add the lemon juice, sugar, nutrient and yeast. Stir well and ferment.

ROSE-HIP WINE

	Imperial	*U.S.*	*Metric*
Rose-hips	3½ lb.	3 lb.	1¾ kilo.
Sugar	3 lb.	2½ lb.	1½ kilo.
Water	1 gallon	1 gallon	5 litres

1 lemon, yeast and nutrient.

Method:

Gather the rose-hips in October. Wash and crush them, add

the sugar and then the boiling water. Stir well and cover. When cool, add the rind and juice of the lemon, the nutrient and the yeast. Ferment on the pulp for a week, then strain and press the hips and continue the ferment.

ROWANBERRY WINE

	Imperial	U.S.	Metric
Rowanberries	5 lb.	4¼ lb.	2½ kilo.
Wheat	1 lb.	14 oz.	½ kilo.
Raisins	2 oz.	2 oz.	60 grams
Root ginger	1 oz.	1 oz.	30 grams
Sugar	3 lb.	2½ lb.	1½ kilo.
Water	1 gallon	1 gallon	5 litres

1 lemon, yeast and nutrient.

Method:

Stalk and rinse the berries, rinse and crush the wheat, chop the raisins, crush the root ginger. Pour on the boiling water, cover and steep for 4 days, stirring twice daily. Strain and press, add the lemon juice, sugar, nutrient and yeast. Stir well and ferment.

SLOE WINE

	Imperial	U.S.	Metric
Sloes	3 lb.	2½ lb.	1½ kilo.
Sugar	3½ lb.	3 lb.	1¾ kilo.
Water	1 gallon	1 gallon	5 litres

Yeast and nutrient.

Method:

Gather sloes in November. Stalk and rinse them, pour on the boiling water, cover and leave for 4 days, stirring twice daily. Strain and press, add sugar, nutrient and yeast, stir well and ferment.

TOMATO WINE

	Imperial	U.S.	Metric
Well-ripened tomatoes	8 lb.	6¾ lb.	4 kilo.
Salt	1 tablesp.	1 tablesp.	1 tablesp.
Bruised root ginger	1 oz.	1 oz.	30 grams
Sugar	3 lb.	2½ lb.	1½ kilo.
Water	1 gallon	1 gallon	5 litres

Yeast and nutrient.

Method:

Dissolve the sugar in boiling water and pour over the tomatoes which have been broken up with your hands. Add the ginger and nutrient and, when cool, the yeast. Ferment on the pulp, pressing down the tomatoes twice daily and keeping the crock well covered. After 14 days, strain and continue the fermentation in a jar.

GRAPE WINES

White Wine. Using pale green grapes

(a) From local grapes. Gather as late as possible, leaving them till the leaves have fallen, if you can. You will need up to 15 lbs. of grapes to make 1 gal. of wine. Crush the fruit, with your hands, but do not crush the pips. Take out the central stems, but leave in the smaller fruit stalks. Add 1 Campden tablet, cover and leave overnight. Next day, strain and press the pulp till it is dry and test the juice with a hydrometer. The reading is likely to be between 1·050 and 1·070. Add sugar to increase the reading to about 1·090 for a dry wine and 1·120 for a medium wine. Remember 2¼ ozs. of sugar will raise the gravity by about 5°. Stir thoroughly and add a fermenting yeast. Continue as indicated in the body of this book.

(b) From imported grapes. The little seedless Cypriot grapes, on sale in stores during August, are excellent for this purpose and quite cheap. A tray of grapes containing 18 lbs. will produce 1½ gals. of juice.

Pick over the grapes, removing the stems and any really mouldy grapes. Loose or brown-edged fruits are all right. Rinse, crush with your hands, add 1 Campden tablet, cover and leave overnight. Next day, strain and press, check the specific gravity of the juice and if need be add a little more sugar. Stir thoroughly, add the fermenting yeast—sherry is strongly recommended—and continue as before.

Red Wine. Use red or black grapes

The differences between local and imported white grapes apply similarly to the red and black grapes and so will not be repeated.

Crush the grapes, remove the stems, add 1 Campden tablet, cover closely and leave overnight. Next day, strain off sufficient juice to test the specific gravity and add sugar as required.

Return the juice to the pulp and stir to dissolve the sugar. Stir in a fermenting yeast and *ferment on the pulp* for 4 or 5 days. Strain and press and continue the fermentation as usual.

N.B. 1. Additional acid is NOT required. Grapes have sufficient. But 1 nutrient tablet per gallon helps to get a really dry wine.

2. If you haven't a hydrometer, add 1¼ lbs. of sugar to local grapes for a dry wine and 2 lbs. of sugar for a medium to sweet wine. For imported grapes additional sugar may not be necessary, unless you are making a strong wine, when a few extra ounces can be added, when the ferment slows down.

3. If you have insufficient imported grapes and decide to add water, also add the juice of a lemon and extra sugar to compensate for the dilution.

4. Local grapes that are not fully ripe and therefore over-acid should be diluted and sweetened, but no lemon juice is required.

Wine from Grape Juice Concentrate

Several firms import from Spain concentrated grape juices—both red and white. The specific gravity of the concentrate is about 1·385 and it has only to be diluted with water and fermented. You can add between 2 and 3 parts of water to 1 of concentrate, according to the type of wine you wish to make. 2 parts water and 1 part concentrate will show a specific gravity of about 1·128, which would make a dry wine of about 17% alcohol or more likely a medium wine of 13% to 15% alcohol. If 3 parts of water are used (and this is the maximum) the resulting specific gravity will be about 1·096; this hould ferment to dryness and produce 12½% alcohol, which is ample in a table wine. Briefly then 2 parts water to 1 part concentrate for a dessert wine. 3 parts of water to 1 part concentrate for a table wine. The juice of 1 large lemon per gallon of must is required to increase the acidity, and of course yeast to your choice.

The concentrate appears to be expensive, but in fact the resulting wine costs little more than 25¢ a bottle. Furthermore it is excellent wine in every way and has a remarkable quality of maturing very quickly. It can in fact be served as little as 6 weeks after starting the ferment, though it will improve if kept longer.

The methods are the same with both white and red concentrates.

VEGETABLE WINES

Generally speaking it is best to use vegetables at the end of their season, provided they are sound and free from disease. Mostly they have to be scrubbed thoroughly, *but not peeled,* diced into ½-in. cubes and boiled gently in an open pan till just tender. Often their flavour is insufficient in itself and herbs or spices are added. Nearly all vegetables are deficient in acid, tannin and yeast nutrient, and so these must be forgotten. The tannin may be added, in the form of 1 tablespoonful of very strong tea, to the finished wine.

ARTICHOKE WINE

	Imperial	U.S.	Metric
Artichokes	4 lb.	3½ lb.	2 kilo.
Root ginger	2 oz.	2 oz.	60 grams
Sugar	3 lb.	2½ lb.	1½ kilo.
Water	1 gallon	1 gallon	5 litres

1 lemon, yeast and nutrient.

Method:

Dice the artichokes, thinly peel the fruit and bruise the ginger. Boil all together for 30 mins., then strain onto the sugar, stir well, cover and allow to cool. Add the nutrient and yeast— sherry for preference—and ferment.

BEETROOT WINE

	Imperial	U.S.	Metric
Beetroot	5 lb.	4½ lb.	2½ kilo.
Sugar	3 lb.	2½ lb.	1½ kilo
Water	1 gallon	1 gallon	5 litres

Yeast and nutrient and 1 large lemon (4 to 6 loves and ½ oz. or 15 grams root ginger may also be added)

Method:

Scrub the beetroot, dice and add to the water together with the thinly pared lemon rind. Bring to the boil and simmer till the beet is just tender and has blanched almost white. Strain off the liquid onto the sugar and stir thoroughly. Cover, and when cool add the lemon juice, nutrient and yeast. Ferment as usual but mature for 2 years or more till the earthy flavour and purple hue have completely disappeared. The cloves and ginger may be added in the boiling if desired.

BROAD BEAN WINE

	Imperial	U.S.	Metric
Old shelled broad beans	4 lb.	3½ lb.	2 kilo.
Raisins	4 oz.	4 oz.	125 grams
Sugar	2¾ lb.	2¼ lb.	1.4 kilo.
Water	1 gallon	1 gallon	5 litres

1 lemon, yeast and nutrient.

Method:

Boil the beans gently for 1 hr., taking care not to allow the skins to break. Strain onto the sugar and chopped raisins; stir well and cover. When cool, add the lemon juice, nutrient and yeast. After a week strain to remove the raisins and continue the fermentation.

CARROT WINE

	Imperial	U.S.	Metric
Carrots	5 lb.	4¼ lb.	2½ kilo.
Wheat	1 lb.	14 oz.	½ kilo.
Sugar	3½ lb.	3 lb.	1¾ kilo.
Water	1 gallon	1 gallon	5 litres

2 lemons, 2 oranges, yeast and nutrient.

Method:

Scrub the carrots, dice and add to the water. Rinse and crush the wheat, pare the oranges and lemons, add these also to the water. Bring to the boil and simmer till the carrots are tender. Strain onto the sugar, stir well and cover. When the must is cool, add the juice only of the oranges and lemons and also the nutrient and yeast, and ferment. This wine also needs long keeping.

CELERY WINE

	Imperial	U.S.	Metric
Celery stalk without leaves	4 lb.	3½ lb.	2 kilo.
Sugar	3 lb.	2½ lb.	1½ kilo.
Water	1 gallon	1 gallon	5 litres

Yeast and nutrient.

Method:

Chop the celery gently, boil till it is just tender, strain onto the sugar, stir well and cover till cool. Add the nutrient and yeast, and ferment as usual. Demerara sugar will add a little colour to the wine.

LETTUCE WINE

	Imperial	U.S.	Metric
Chopped lettuce, excluding any bad outside leaves	2½ lb.	2 lb.	1¼ kilo.
Raisins	8 oz.	7 oz.	¼ kilo.
Wheat	8 oz.	7 oz.	¼ kilo.
Sugar	3 lb.	2½ lb.	1½ kilo.
Water	1 gallon	1 gallon	5 litres
Yeast and nutrient.			

Method:

Simmer the lettuce in the water and strain onto the sugar, chopped raisins, crushed wheat, rinds of the orange and lemon. Stir well and cover. When cool, add the orange and lemon juice, nutrient and yeast. Ferment for a week, strain and press and continue the fermentation.

MANGOLD WINE

	Imperial	U.S.	Metric
Sugar	5 lb.	4¼ lb.	2½ kilo.
Water	3 lb.	2½ lb.	1½ kilo.
Mangolds	1 gallon	1 gallon	5 litres
2 lemons, 2 oranges, yeast and nutrient.			

Method:

Scrub and dice the mangolds, boil until tender. Strain into the sugar and fruit rinds, stir and cover. When cool, add the fruit juice, nutrient and yeast, and ferment.

MARROW WINE

	Imperial	U.S.	Metric
A ripe marrow, about	5 lb.	4¼ lb.	2½ kilo.
Sugar	3 lb.	2½ lb.	1½ kilo.
Water	1 gallon	1 gallon	5 litres
Ginger (optional)	1 oz.	1 oz.	30 grams
2 oranges, 2 lemons, yeast and nutrient.			

Method:

Wipe the marrow clean and grate it coarsely into a vessel. Include the seeds, the fruit rinds and the bruised ginger. Pour on the boiling water, stir well and cover. When cool, add the fruit juices, nutrient and yeast. Cover and leave for 5 days, stirring twice daily. Strain and press and continue the fermentation.

PARSLEY WINE

	Imperial	U.S.	Metric
Fresh parsley leaves, picked early in the season (or 1 packet dried parsley)	1 lb.	14 oz.	½ kilo.
Sugar	3 lb.	2½ lb.	1½ kilo.
Barley	1 lb.	14 oz.	½ kilo.
Water	1 gallon	1 gallon	5 litres
Bruised ginger	½ oz.	½ oz.	15 grams

2 oranges, 2 lemons, yeast and nutrient.

Method:

Boil the parsley, bruised ginger and thin peelings of the oranges and lemons for 20 mins. Dried parsley should be soaked for 24 hrs. beforehand. Strain onto sugar and crushed barley, stir well and cover. When cool, add the fruit juice, nutrient and yeast. 1 week later strain and continue the fermentation.

PARSNIP WINE

	Imperial	U.S.	Metric
Parsnips, prepared	4 lb.	3½ lb.	2 kilo.
Sugar	3 lb.	2½ lb.	1½ kilo.
Water	1 gallon	1 gallon	

2 oranges, 2 lemons, yeast and nutrient.

Method:

Scrub and dice the parsnips, removing rusty parts in the process. Add the fruit rinds and gently boil till just tender. Strain onto the sugar. Stir well and cover. When cool, add the fruit juice, nutrient and yeast, and ferment as usual.

PEA POD WINE

	Imperial	U.S.	Metric
Pea pods	5 lb.	4½ lb.	2½ kilo.
Sugar	3 lb.	2½ lb.	1½ kilo.
Water	1 gallon	1 gallon	5 litres

Yeast and nutrient.

Method:

Use sound, clean, fresh pods and boil gently till they are tender. Strain onto the sugar, stir well and cover. When cool, add the nutrient and yeast, and ferment as usual.

POTATO WINE

	Imperial	U.S.	Metric
Old potatoes	5 lb.	4¼ lb.	2½ kilo.
Sugar	3 lb.	2½ lb.	1½ kilo.
Water	1 gallon	1 gallon	5 litres

2 lemons, 2 oranges, yeast and nutrient.

Method:

Scrub and dice the potatoes, add the fruit rinds and boil till just tender; strain onto sugar, stir well and cover. When cool, add the fruit juice, nutrient and yeast.

This is a "minimum requirements" recipe. Potatoes are not by themselves very suitable for winemaking since they lack flavour and produce a proportion of wood alcohol. Potatoes are in fact better used in conjunction with other ingredients. The following recipe is, therefore recommended:

OLD POTATOES

	Imperial	U.S.	Metric
Old potatoes	2 lb.	1¾ lb.	1 kilo.
Raisins	1 lb.	14 oz.	½ kilo.
Barley or wheat	1 lb.	14 oz.	½ kilo.
Sugar	3 lb.	2½ lb.	1½ kilo.
Water	1 gallon	1 gallon	5 litres

1 lemon, yeast and nutrient.

Method:

Scrub and dice the potatoes or better still grate them coarsely. Chop the raisins and crush the barley or wheat, pare the lemon and put the rind and other dry ingredients in a vessel with the sugar. Pour the boiling water over them, stir well and cover. When cool, add the lemon juice, nutrient and yeast. Ferment on the pulp for 8 days, strain and press and continue the ferment.

SPINACH WINE

	Imperial	U.S.	Metric
Spinach	2½ lb.	2 lb.	1¼ kilo.
Raisins	1 lb.	14 oz.	½ kilo.
Sugar	3 lb.	2½ lb.	1½ kilo.
Water	1 gallon	1 gallon	5 litres

1 lemon, 1 orange, yeast and nutrient.

Method:

Chop and boil the spinach for 30 mins. and strain onto the sugar, fruit rinds and chopped raisins; stir well and cover. When cool, add the fruit juice, nutrient and yeast. Strain off the raisins 7 days later and continue the fermentation.

MISCELLANEOUS WINES

Birch Sap Wine

N.B. 1. Sap should only be taken from mature birch trees, i.e. with a diameter of 9 ins. or more.

2. Sap should only be taken during the first two weeks in March when the sap is rising.

3. The hole should be bored no more than 1 in. or thereabouts, i.e. to just beyond the inside of the bark.

4. After use the hole should be plugged tightly with a sound cork. *Failure to observe these points may damage the tree irreparably.*

5. The hole should be bored about 15 ins. from the ground, slanting slightly upwards to enable the sap to drain *down* the hole.

6. The diameter of the hole should be the same as the diameter of the rubber or plastic tube that you will use for drainage of the tree.

7. Drill your hole, insert your tube with the other end in a gallon jar. Cover with a cloth and leave for 2 days. By this time the jar should be full or nearly so. Leave another day if necessary.

INGREDIENTS:

	Imperial	*U.S.*	*Metric*
Birch sap	1 gallon	1 gallon	5 litres
Raisins	8 oz.	7 oz.	¼ kilo.
Sugar	3 lb.	2½ lb.	1½ liko.

2 lemons, 2 oranges, yeast and nutrient.

Method:

Thinly peel the fruit, add to the sap and bring to the boil and simmer for 20 mins. Add cold water to restore that lost in boiling and pour onto the sugar and broken raisins. Stir well and cover. When cool, add the fruit juice, nutrient and yeast. After 1 week, strain and continue the fermentation.

Sycamore, maple and walnut sap wines can also be made in the same way.

GINGER WINE

Root ginger	2 oz.	2 oz.	60 grams
Raisins	8 oz.	7 oz.	¼ kilo.
Sugar	3 lb.	2½ lb.	1½ kilo.
Water	1 gallon	1 gallon	5 litres

2 lemons, 2 oranges, yeast and nutrient.

Method:

Boil the well-bruised ginger and thinly pared fruit rinds for ½ hr. Pour onto the sugar and broken raisins, stir well and cover. When cool, add the fruit juice, nutrient and yeast. After 1 week, strain and continue the fermentation.

CORN WINE

	Imperial	*U.S.*	*Metric*
Crushed corn	1½ lb.	1¼ lb.	¾ kilo.
Raisins	1 lb.	14 oz.	½ kilo.
Sugar	3 lb.	2½ lb.	1½ kilo.
Water	1 gallon	1 gallon	5 litres

2 lemons, 2 oranges, yeast and nutrient.

Method:

Soak the corn overnight in some of the water to soften it and next day crush it in a coarse mincer, together with the raisins. Thinly peel the oranges and lemons; mix them with the corn and raisins, add the sugar and pour on the boiling water. Stir thoroughly and cover. When cool, add the nutrient, fruit juices and yeast. Ferment all together for 10 days, then strain without pressing and continue the fermentation.

RICE WINE

	Imperial	*U.S.*	*Metric*
Coarsely crushed rice	1 lb.	14 oz.	½ kilo.
Chopped raisins	1 lb.	14 oz.	½ kilo.
Sugar	3 lb.	2½ lb.	1½ kilo.
Water	1 gallon	1 gallon	5 litres

1 lemon, yeast and nutrient.

Method:

Pour boiling water onto the rice, sugar, raisins and thinly peeled skin of the lemon. Stir well and cover. When cool, add the lemon juice, nutrient and yeast, and ferment all together for 1 week, stirring twice daily and keeping the crock well covered, strain without pressing. Continue to ferment.

TEA WINE

	Imperial	*U.S.*	*Metric*
Cold tea	1 gallon	1 gallon	5 litres
Chopped raisins	1 lb.	14 oz.	½ kilo.
Sugar	3 lb.	2½ lb.	1½ kilo.

2 lemons, 2 oranges, yeast and nutrient.

Method:

Save tea left over from the teapot until you have a gallon. Add the raisins, thinly pared fruit skins, fruit juice, sugar, nutrient and yeast. Stir well and ferment for 1 week; then strain, press, and continue the fermentation.

WHEAT WINE

	Imperial	*U.S.*	*Metric*
Wheat	1½ lb.	1¼ lb.	¾ kilo.
Raisins	2 lb.	1¾ lb.	1 kilo.
Sugar	3 lb.	2½ lb.	1½ kilo.
Water	1 gallon	1 gallon	5 litres

2 lemons, 2 oranges, yeast and nutrient.

Method:

Crush the wheat, chop the raisins and mix with the sugar and the thinly peeled fruit skins. Pour on the boiling water, stir well and cover. When cool add the fruit juice, nutrient and yeast. Ferment for 1 week, strain without pressing and continue the fermentation.

GENERAL INDEX

INDEX OF WINE RECIPES

Recipes for cider, perry, etc., will be found in their place in the General Index